CW00516779

PIKETTY

MARX AND

CAPITAL

PRASANNA CHOUDHARY

©PRASANNA CHOUDHARY 2014

Piketty Marx and Capital by Prasanna Choudhary

CONTENTS

1. APOCALYPSE AND EXUBERANCE

No. This is not a story about London society where 'old Madame du Deffand and her friends talked for fifty years without stopping, and during those fifty years Madame du Deffand said no more than three witty things (or that the fraction of three witty sayings lasted eighteen thousand two hundred and fifty nights).'[1]

This is also not a story about the *Faubourg Saint-Germain*, about 'Princesse de Guermantes's drawing room, illuminated, forgetful, and flowery, like a peaceful cemetery, where time had not only brought about the ruin of the creatures of a former epoch, it had made possible, had indeed created, new associations.'[2]

This is about a sanatorium. In Davos, Switzerland. News of the assassination of a prince in not very far off Sarajevo was still in the making.

AN OLD STORY RETOLD

Tubercular patients from all over the world in the International Sanatorium Berghof formed a 'charmed circle of isolation and invalidism', and 'in a sort of substitute existence', spent their time talking of disease and health; life, love and death; civilization and humanity's prospects, etc. Two of them got engaged in very intense arguments over the future of capitalism, of bourgeois democracy.

One was **Ludovico Settembrini**, a literary man, the rhetorical rationalist and humanist, grandson of a Milanese lawyer, a patriot, political agitator, orator and journalist Giuseppe Settembrini. He is quite excited about the prospect of bourgeois democracy's victorious march all over the world.

He was also a **Freemason**. He had much to tell of the great names whose bearers had been Masons: Voltaire, Lafayette, Napoleon, Franklin and Washington, Mazzini and Garibaldi; among the living, the King of England, and besides him, a large group of people in whose hands lay the conduct of nations of Europe, members of governments and parliaments.

His exuberance was well reflected in his arguments: "Technical progress gradually subjugated nature, by developing roads and telegraphs, minimizing climatic differences; and by the means of communication which it created proved itself the most reliable agents in the task of drawing together the peoples of the earth, of making them acquainted with each other, of building bridges to compromise, of destroying prejudice; of finally, bringing about the universal brotherhood of man. Humanity had sprung from the depths of fear, darkness and hatred: but it was emerging, it was moving onward and upward, toward a goal of fellow-feeling and enlightenment, of goodness and joyousness; and upon this path, the industrial arts were the vehicle conducive to the greatest progress. ....Christ had been the first to proclaim the principle of equality and union, that the printing-press had propagated the doctrine, and that finally the French Revolution had elevated it into a law. ....

The achievements wrung from the past by the Renaissance and the intellectual revival, are personality, freedom, and the rights of man. ....

Two principles were in perpetual conflict for possession of the world: force and justice, tyranny and freedom, superstition and knowledge. ....There was no doubt as to which of the two would finally triumph; it would be the power of enlightenment, the power that made for rational advance and development. For human progress snatched up ever more peoples with it on its brilliant course; it conquered more and more territory in Europe itself and was already pressing Asia-wards. Much still remained to be done, sublime exertions were still demanded from those spirits who had received the light. Then only the day would come when thrones would crash and outworn religions crumble, in those remaining countries of Europe which had not already enjoyed the blessings of eighteenth century enlightenment, nor yet of an upheaval like 1789. But the day would come if not on the wings of dove, then on the pinion of eagles; and dawn would break over Europe, the dawn of universal brotherhood, in the name of justice, science, and human reason. It would bring in its train a new Holy Alliance, the alliance of the democratic peoples of Europe. .... In a word, it would bring in its train the republic of the world. ...."[3]

The other was **Leo Naphta**, professor of ancient languages, son of a village slaughterer father and a working class mother. His mother worked in a cotton-spinning factory, where she labored as long as her strength held out, while the children attended the common school. Naphta, in his young age, studied **Karl Marx**'s '**Capital**' in a cheap edition, and passed from Karl Marx to **Hegel**. Born a Jew, he converted to the Roman Catholic faith and 'sang the praises of the Middle Ages'.

He became a **Jesuit**.

He was convinced of the apocalyptic end of capitalism. He, too, was quite forthright in defense of his conviction: "Is your Manchester liberalism unaware of the existence of a school of economic thought which means the triumph of man over economics, and whose principles and aims precisely coincides with those of the kingdom of God? ....The fathers of the Church ....were humane enough, anti-commercial enough, to feel that all commercial activity was a danger to the soul of man and its salvation. They hated money and finance, and called the empire of capital fuel for the fires of the hell. The fundamental economic principle that price is regulated by the operation of the law of supply and demand, they have always despised from the bottom of their hearts; and condemned taking advantage of chance as a cynical exploitation of a neighbor's need. Even more nefarious, in their eyes, was the exploitation of time; the monstrousness of receiving a premium for the passage of time – interest, in other words – and misusing to one's own advantage and another's disadvantage a universal and God-given dispensation. ....Quite indeed, these humane spirits were revolted by the idea of the automatic increase of money; they regarded as usury every kind of interest-taking and speculation, and declared that every rich man was either a thief or the heir of a thief. They went further. Like **Thomas Aquinas**, they considered trade, pure and simple, buying and selling for profit, without altering or improving the product, a contemptible occupation. .... They demanded that the measure of profit or of public esteem should be in proportion to the actual labor expended, and accordingly it was not the tradesman or the industrialist, but the laborer and the tiller of the soil, who were honorable in their eyes. For, they were in favor of making production dependent upon necessity, and held mass production in abhorrence.

Now then: after centuries of disfavor these principles and standards are being resurrected by the modern movement of communism. The similarity is complete, even to the claim for world-domination made by international labor as against international industry and finance; the world-proletariat, which is today asserting the ideal of the *Civitas Dei* in opposition to the discredited and decadent standards of the capitalistic bourgeoisie. The dictatorship of the proletariat, the politico-economic means of salvation demanded by our age, does not mean domination for its own sake and in perpetuity; but rather in the sense of a temporary abrogation, in the Sign of the Cross, of the contradiction between spirit and force; in the sense of overcoming the world by mastering it; in a transcendental, a transitional sense, in the sense of the Kingdom. ....

What had been the net result of the vainglorious French Revolution – what but the capitalistic bourgeois state? ..Progress? It was the cry of the patient who constantly changes his position thinking each new one will bring relief. ..The flabby humanitarianism of it went hand in hand with the wolfish cruelty and baseness of the economic conflict within the bourgeois state. War, war! ..Justice, in short, was an empty husk, stock-in-trade of bourgeois rhetoric. ..Freedom is historically bound up with the inhuman degeneration of commercial morality, with all the horrors of modern industrialism and speculation, and with the devilish domination of money and finance...."[4]

These passionate arguments led them to duel with pistols. Settembrini refused to fire at Naphta; instead he fired in the air. Naphta shot himself in the head, leaving behind the blackened red hole in the temple.

Naphta died; Settembrini with his excessive fondness for fairy tale capitalism survived. But soon, there 'came the peal of thunder, that deafening explosion of long-gathering magazines of passion and spleen; that historic thunder-peal made the foundations of the earth to shake; and that fired the mine beneath the magic mountain.' The First World War had begun.

In between these arguments, **Hans Castorp**, young scion of good Hamburg society, and an indifferent engineer, although sympathetically inclined towards Settembrini's views, often pondered over striking a balance, a pedagogic equilibrium, a sort of harmony.

I do not intend to stay further in the magical world of **Thomas Mann**. I can now descend from the magic mountain to the flatland of real life existence.

Davos now hosts the World Economic Forum's annual gathering of corporate bigwigs, heads of governments, and who's who of the world. They discuss the health of global capitalism.

MARX AND KUZNETS

Almost a century after the story stated above, **Thomas Piketty**, in his **'Capital in the Twenty-First Century'**[5], strives to tread the path between, what he calls, 'the two extremes of **Marxian apocalypse** and **Simon Kuznets**'s **excessive fondness for fairy tales, or at any rate happy endings.**' This theme runs throughout the book. He does not believe in Kuznets's fairy tales, and the thrust of his study is on avoiding Marxian apocalypse.

Whether Karl Marx's analysis of capitalism can be categorized as 'apocalyptic' or not will be dealt with in course of the critique. So far as Kuznets's study is concerned, it was, from the very beginning, lacking in credibility. At the beginning of the Cold War in early fifties of the last century, when McCarthyism was at its height in the United States, Simon Kuznets's findings were part of a political project to counter Soviet communism. It was designed to present a rosy picture of capitalism – it tried to show that inequality was not an inalienable part of capitalism, that over the course of industrialization and economic development inequality actually decreases, and this trend (reduction of inequality) was in fact observed in the US between 1913 and 1948. He further portrayed this finding 'as one instance of a more general phenomenon, which should theoretically reproduce itself everywhere, including underdeveloped countries then mired in post-colonial poverty.'

Piketty rightly points out, "The sharp reduction in income inequality that we observe in almost all the rich countries between 1914 and 1945 was due above all to the world wars and the violent economic and political shocks they entailed. ….It has little to do with the tranquil process of inter-sector mobility described by Kuznets. ….The data Kuznets had presented in his 1953 book suddenly became a powerful political weapon. He was well aware of the highly speculative nature of his theorizing. ..He took care to remind his listeners that the intent of his optimistic predictions was quite simply to maintain the underdeveloped countries 'within the orbit of the free world'. In large part, then, the theory of the Kuznets curve was a product of the Cold War." Kuznets himself put it: 'This is perhaps 5% empirical information and 95% speculation, some of it possibly tainted by wishful thinking.' (Piketty, 'Introduction/The Kuznets Curve') Despite these clear-cut observations, one wonders why Piketty gives so much space and importance to Kuznets.

While Piketty is quite forthright regarding Kuznets's exuberance, he appears to be quite defensive about 'Marxian apocalypse'. He writes, "Despite ….limitations, Marx's analysis remains relevant in several respects. First, he began with an important question (concerning the unprecedented concentration of wealth during the Industrial Revolution) and tried to answer it with the means at his disposal, economists today would do well to take inspiration from his example. Even more important, the principle of infinite accumulation that Marx proposed contains a key insight, as valid for the study of the twenty-first century as it was for the nineteenth and in some respects more worrisome than **Ricardo**'s principle of scarcity. If the rates of population and productivity growth are relatively low, then accumulated wealth naturally takes on considerable importance, especially if it grows to extreme proportions, and becomes socially destabilizing. In other words, low growth cannot adequately counterbalance the Marxist principle of infinite accumulation: the resulting equilibrium is not as apocalyptic as the one predicted by Marx but is nevertheless quite disturbing. Accumulation ends at a finite level, but that level may be high enough to be destabilizing. In particular, the very high level of private wealth that has been attained since the 1980s and 1990s in the wealthy countries of Europe and in Japan, measured in years of national income, directly reflects the Marxist logic." ('Introduction/Marx: The Principle of Infinite Accumulation'. Here I would like to replace the word 'infinite' with 'unsustainable' – unsustainable accumulation. Although Marx uses terms like 'endless' or 'limitless', this should be understood in conjunction with his theory of periodic cycle of crisis and social revolution. Its un-sustainability makes it what Piketty calls 'socially destabilizing'.) So much so for Apocalypse and Happy Endings! Let Princess Apocalypse and Mademoiselle Exuberance amuse themselves in their respective salons. I can now move on.

2. DATA AND DIALECTICS

France inherits a very rich and glorious intellectual-theoretical tradition. Beginning with **Michel de Montaigne** (1533-1592) and **René Descartes** (1596-1650), this tradition includes leading lights of French Enlightenment like, to name a few, **Charles Louis de Montesquieu** (1689-1755), **François Voltaire** (1694-1778), **Jean-Jacques Rousseau** (1712-1778), **Denis Diderot** (1713-1784), and **Jean Antoine Condorcet** (1743-1794). The French Enlightenment played a vital role in the making of modern mind. Marx's methodology too was indebted to these great minds. This tradition was carried forward by later French thinkers as well. Even in the twentieth century, **F Saussure** and **Claude Lévi-Strauss** pioneered structuralism in linguistics and anthropology respectively. **Jean Paul-Satre** influenced a whole generation of intellectuals as well as activists. **Simone de Beauvoir**'s 'The Second Sex' became the guiding spirit behind the feminist movement. **Émile Durkheim** and his theories and hypotheses became an integral part of social science studies the world over. '**Annales School**' found a large audience among the historians, and its clones emerged in various universities around the world. These are just a few names; it is not possible here to give even a brief description of France's immense contribution to the intellectual wealth of humankind and their vital role in the evolution of the theory of knowledge. Many of these thinkers were system-builders and versatile genius – Descartes himself was one of the founders of analytical geometry, mathematician, physicist, physiologist, philosopher and founder of rationalism.

In this background, it is quite understandable that young Piketty's dream was 'to teach at the **École des Hautes Études en Sciences Sociales,** whose faculty has included such leading lights as **Lucien Febvre, Fernand Braudel,** Claude Lévi-Strauss, **Pierre Bourdieu, Françoise Héritier,** and **Maurice Godelier,** to name a few…' He further writes, "There is one great advantage to being an academic economist in France: here economists are not highly respected in the academic and intellectual world or by political and financial elites. Hence they must set aside their contempt for other disciplines and their absurd claim to greater scientific legitimacy, despite the fact that they know almost nothing about anything. …." Explaining his theoretical and conceptual framework, Piketty strongly criticizes 'childish passion for mathematics .. at the expense of historical research and collaboration with other social sciences.' 'Economists are all too often preoccupied with petty mathematical problems of interest only to themselves. This obsession with mathematics is an easy way of acquiring the appearance of scientificity without having to answer the far more complex questions posed by the world we live in.' Finally, he makes clear the aim behind his study – he wants to 'contribute, however modestly, to the debate about the best way to organize society and the most appropriate institutions and policies to achieve a just social order.' Furthermore, he 'would like to see justice achieved effectively and efficiently under the rule of law, which should apply equally to all and derive from universally

understood statutes subject to democratic debate.'
('Introduction/The Theoretical and Conceptual
Framework') Well said, indeed.

BIG DATA METHODOLOGY

However, despite his somewhat emotional fondness for the
French intellectual tradition and French theoreticians, his
criticism of 'childish passion for mathematics', and his
eagerness to collaborate with the other social sciences,
Piketty, so far as the main theme of the book is concerned,
follows the **'big data methodology'**. (His book is not a big
data book in the strict sense of the term – what I am
referring to is his methodology.) He appears to be
consciously avoiding **'why'**, and remains content to explain
'what'. He tells us 'what' the data (spread over a very long
period of two centuries) reveals about the movement of
inequality in the age of capital (i.e., r > g), but he desists
from going into the question 'why' r > g. He does not
critically examine existing hypotheses or theories on this
question, and he himself does not advance any hypothesis
or theory in this regard, and hence, does not put such
hypothesis or theory to test in the light of appropriate data.
In short, he deliberately avoids venturing into the field of
hypotheses or theories or reasoning – he is satisfied with
correlations, and does not feel the need of **causal
analyses**.

'With a cell phone in every pocket, a computer in every
backpack, and big information technology systems in back
offices everywhere', the digital age has made it quite easy
to generate, store, process and retrieve large amounts of
data at a scale previously unheard-of. "In the analog age

collecting and analyzing such data was enormously costly and time-consuming. New questions often meant that the data had to be collected again and the analysis started afresh. The big step toward managing data more efficiently came with the advent of digitization: making analog information readable by computers, which also makes it easier and cheaper to store and process. ....**Google** processes more than 24 petabytes of data per day, a volume that is thousands of times the quantity of all printed material in the US Library of Congress. **Facebok**, a company that did not exist a decade ago, gets more than 10 million new photos uploaded every hour. Facebook members click a 'like' button or leave a comment nearly three billion times per day, creating a digital trail that the company can mine to learn about users' preferences. Meanwhile, the 800 million users of Google's **YouTube** service upload over an hour of video every second. The number of messages on **Twitter** grows at around 200 percent a year and by 2012 had exceeded 400 million tweets a day. ....In 2013 the amount of stored information in the world is estimated to be around 1,200 exabytes (an exabyte is one billion gigabytes), of which less than 2 percent is non-digital. ....**The era of big data challenges the way we live and interact with the world. Most strikingly, society will need to shed some of its obsession for causality in exchange for simple correlations: not knowing *why* but only *what*. This overturns centuries of established practices and challenges our most basic understanding of how to make decisions and comprehend reality. ....By changing the amount, we change the essence.** ....The change of scale has led to a change of state. ....The quantitative change has led to a qualitative one. ... **As we transition from a *hypothesis-driven* world to a *data-driven* world, we may be tempted to think that we also no longer need theories**."[6]

"In 2008 **WIRED** magazine's editor-in-chief **Chris Anderson** trumpeted that 'the data deluge makes the scientific method obsolete.' In a cover story called 'The Petabyte Age', he proclaimed that it amounted to nothing short of 'the end of theory'. The traditional process of scientific discovery – of a hypothesis that is tested against reality using a model of underlying causalities – is on its way out, Anderson argued, replaced by statistical analysis of pure correlations that is devoid of theory.'[7] Piketty rightly acknowledges his indebtedness to 'recent improvements in the technology of research', but, I hope, he does not subscribe to Anderson's views.

However, the big data experts **Viktor Mayer-Schönberger** and **Kenneth Cukier** do not view analogs and algorithms, causality and correlation, 'why' and 'what' as dichotomous categories. They admit that big data itself is founded on theory (statistical theories, mathematical, computer science theories), and big data analysis is based on theories (how we select the data). 'They shape both our methods and our results.' They conclude, "We still need causal studies and controlled experiments with carefully curated data in certain cases. ....But for many everyday needs, knowing what not why is good enough. And big data correlations can point the way toward promising areas in which to explore causal relationships."[8]

AMARTYA SEN'S METHODOLOGY

Amartya Sen who also grapples with the problem of inequality, justice and democracy in our modern world, derives his inspiration from the French Enlightenment. His methodology traces its origin to the 'social choice theory' (of Condorcet in the eighteenth century) which has been developed in the present form by the pioneering contributions of **Kenneth Arrow** in the mid-twentieth century (Condorcet → Kenneth Arrow → Amartya Sen). He critically examines **John Rawls**'s theory of justice, while developing his own views and propositions. Tracing the genesis of his own theory, he writes, " There is a substantial dichotomy between two different lines of reasoning about justice that can be seen among two groups of leading philosophers associated with the radical thought of the Enlightenment period. One approach concentrated on identifying perfectly just social arrangements, and took the characterization of 'just institutions' to be the principal – and often the only identified – task of the theory of justice. Woven in different ways around the idea of hypothetical 'social contract', major contributions were made in this line of thinking by **Thomas Hobbes** in the seventeenth century, and later by **John Locke**, Jean-Jacques Rousseau and **Immanuel Kant**, among others. The contrarian approach has been the dominant influence in contemporary political philosophy, particularly since a pioneering paper ('Justice As Fairness') in 1958 by John Rawls which preceded his definitive statement on that approach in his classic book, 'A Theory of Justice'.

In contrast, a number of other Enlightenment philosophers (**Smith**, **Condorcet**, **Wollstonecraft**, **Bentham**, **Marx**, **John Stuart Mill**, for example) took a variety of approaches that shared a common interest in making comparisons between different ways in which people's lives may be led, influenced by institutions but also by people's actual behavior, social interactions and other significant determinants. This book ('The Idea of Justice') draws to a great extent on that alternative tradition. The analytical – and rather mathematical – discipline of 'social choice theory', which can be traced to the works of Condorcet in the eighteenth century, but which has been developed in the present form by the pioneering contributions of Kenneth Arrow in the mid-twentieth century, belongs to this second line of investigation. That approach, suitably adapted, can make a substantial contribution …. to addressing questions about the enhancement of justice and the removal of injustice in the world."[9] Thus, Sen talking about the dichotomy between **'transcendental institutionalism'** (or an **'arrangement-focused view of justice'**) and **'realization-focused comparison'** (or **'realization-focused understanding of justice'**) follows the latter line of reasoning. (However, the way Sen classifies Enlightenment philosophers into two opposing camps seems to be somewhat arbitrary.) Since Piketty mentions Sen only in the passing, I will not expand this discussion on Sen's methodology further.

DIALECTICAL METHOD

Here, it will be sufficient to mention that in the dichotomy between 'why' and 'what', causality and correlation, analog and algorithm, Piketty chooses the latter, thereby misses the opportunity to pursue the **dialectical method** in order to grasp why **and** what, causality **and** correlation, analog **and** algorithm **in their interconnections, in their motion and constantly changing places, and in their interpenetration**. He falls prey to the method that views opposing categories in irreconcilable, absolute terms – why versus what, causality versus correlation, analog versus algorithm (and in case of Sen 'arrangement-focused view of justice' versus 'realization-focused understanding of justice'). He thus departs from the great French tradition that played a vital role in the development of the **science of thought**. Descartes was himself a 'brilliant exponent of dialectics', and Rousseau ('Discourse on the Origin of Inequality Among Men') and Diderot ('Rameau's Nephew') produced 'masterpieces of dialectics'.[10]

The genealogy of big data methodology can well be traced back to John Locke's empiricism, and then to **Auguste Comte**'s positivism, to **William James**'s pragmatism, and to **John Dewey**'s instrumentalism (not to mention various shades of twentieth-century positivism). **Big data methodology is, in fact, digital-age avatar of above-mentioned philosophical tradition.**[11]

It seems that 'his vaccination for life, at the age of eighteen (when the Berlin Wall fell) against the conventional but lazy rhetoric of anti-capitalism' went much deeper, creating mistrust of theories and hypotheses; and this mistrust and prejudice was further reinforced when, at the age of twenty-two, he 'experienced the American dream' at Boston.

To be fair to Piketty, it must be mentioned that the quintessential French intellectual (as distinct from the American) asserts and shines forth occasionally in different chapters of the book, particularly when he passionately deals with the Euro-zone crisis and comes out with a number of propositions and proposals.

The role of data should not be underestimated. Piketty's study of the 'World Top Income Database' (WTID, based on the joint work of some thirty researchers around the world) and his findings which form the main content of the book, are definitely major contributions towards understanding income inequality in our time. However, since capital is a network of social relationships, to explore **distributive injustice** (why) is as much, and more so, important as the data-based movement of **income inequality** (what).

To sum up, so far as the methodology of Piketty is concerned, **his pious wish to resurrect the spirit of classical political economy on the one hand, and his pragmatic preference for the big data methodology on the other hand, constitute the first major inconsistency of the book.**

HISTORY: CONTINUITY AND INTERRUPTION

Before moving ahead, a little more on the question of methodology will not be out of context. Piketty rightly suggests that his book can be read as a history book as well. Here, a brief reference from **Michel Foucault** seems relevant: "For many years now historians have preferred to turn their attention to long periods, as if, beneath the shifts and changes of political events, they were trying to reveal the stable, almost indestructible system of checks and balances, the irreversible processes, the constant re-adjustments, the underlying tendencies that gather force, and are then suddenly reversed after centuries of continuity, the movements of accumulation and slow saturation, the great silent, motionless bases that traditional history has covered with a thick layer of events. The tools that enable historians to carry out this work of analysis are partly inherited and partly of their own making: models of economic growth, quantitative analysis of market movements, accounts of demographic expansion and contraction, the study of climate and its long-term changes, the fixing of sociological constants, the description of technological adjustments and of their spread and continuity. These tools have enabled workers in the historical field to distinguish various sedimentary strata; linear successions, which for so long had been the object of research, have given way to discoveries in depth. ....

At about the same time, in the disciplines that we call the history of ideas, the history of science, the history of philosophy, the history of thought, and the history of literature (we can ignore their specificity for the moment), in those disciplines which, despite their names, evade very largely the work and methods of the historians, attention has been turned, on the contrary, away from vast unities like 'periods' or 'centuries' to the phenomenon of rupture, of discontinuity. ....One is now trying to detect the incidence of interruptions. ....They suspend the continuous accumulation of knowledge, interrupt its slow development and force it to enter a new time, cut it off from its empirical origin and its original motivations, cleanse it of its imaginary complicity; they direct historical analysis away from the search for silent beginnings, and the never-ending tracing back to the original precursors, towards the search for a **new type of rationality** and its various effects. There are 'displacements' and 'transformations' of concepts; ..they show that the history of a concept is not wholly and entirely that of its progressive refinement, its continuously increasing rationality, its abstract gradient, but that of its various fields of constitution and validity, that of its successive rules of use, that of the many theoretical contexts in which it developed and matured. .."[12]

Any study of capital in the twenty-first century required the '**architectonic unity**' of both the methods described above by Foucault, but Piketty obviously avoids to 'enter a new time', to search for a 'new type of rationality', and to attempt 'displacements' and 'transformations' of concepts, thereby creating architectural fault-lines in the book which I will deal with in course of this critique.

3. CAPITAL SOCIAL AND SELF-EXPANDING

MONEY IS NOW PREGNANT. Goethe, 'Faust', Part I, Scene5.[13]

Let me begin with Thomas Piketty's definition of capital, labor and 'return on capital'. After all, 'capital' and 'return on capital' form the basic theme of the book.

Piketty writes, "In this book, capital is defined as the sum total of nonhuman assets that can be owned and exchanged on some market. Capital includes all forms of real property (including real estate) as well as financial and professional capital (plants, infrastructure, machinery, patents and so on) used by firms and government agencies. ….Nonhuman capital which in this book I will call simply 'capital', includes all forms of wealth that individuals (or groups of individuals) can own and that can be transferred or traded through the market on a permanent basis. In practice, capital can be owned by private individuals (in which case we speak of 'private capital') or by the government or government agencies (in which case we speak of 'public capital'). There are also intermediate forms. ….Capital is not an immutable concept: it reflects the state of development and prevailing social relations of each society. ….

Throughout this book, when I speak of 'capital' without further qualification, I always exclude what economists often call (unfortunately, to my mind) 'human capital', which consists of an individual's labor-power, skills training, and abilities. ....There are many reasons for excluding human capital from our definition of capital. The most obvious is that human capital cannot be owned by another person or traded on a market (not permanently at any rate). This is a key difference from other forms of capital. One can of course put one's labor services up for hire under a labor contract of some sort. In all modern legal systems, however, such an arrangement has to be limited in both time and scope. In slave societies, of course, this is obviously not true: there, a slaveholder can fully and completely own the human capital of another person and even of that person's offspring. In such societies, slaves can be bought and sold on the market and conveyed by inheritance, and it is common to include slaves in calculating a slaveholder's wealth. I will show how this worked when I examine the composition of private capital in the southern United States before 1865. Leaving such special (and for now historical) cases aside, it makes little sense to attempt to add human and nonhuman capital. ....

I use the words 'capital' and wealth interchangeably. To summarize, I define 'national wealth' or 'national capital' as the total market value of everything, owned by the residents and government of a given country at a given point of time, provided that it can be traded on some market. It consists of the sum total of nonfinancial assets (land, dwellings, commercial inventory, other buildings, machinery, infrastructure, patents, and other directly owned professional assets) and financial assets (bank accounts, mutual funds, bonds, stocks, financial investment of all kinds, insurance policies, pension funds, etc.), less the total amount of financial liabilities (debt). ....

Capital is a stock. It corresponds to the total wealth owned at a given point of time. This stock comes from the wealth appropriated or accumulated in all prior years combined. ...." (Chapter One/Income and Output)

Piketty includes top managers and entrepreneurs in the category of labor, and thus, high salaries paid to them are accounted in the category of labor income.

On the rate of return on capital, he writes, "The rate of return on capital is a central concept in many economic theories. In particular, Marxist analysis emphasizes the falling rate of profit – a historical prediction that turned out to be quite wrong, although it does contain an interesting intuition. The concept of the rate of return on capital also plays a central role in many other theories. In any case, the rate of return on capital measures the yield on capital over the course of a year regardless of its legal form (profits, rents, interest, dividend, royalties, capital gains, etc.), expressed as percentage of the value of capital invested. It is therefore a broader notion than the rate of 'profit', and much broader than the 'rate of interest', while incorporating both." (Chapter One/ Income and Output)

"By construction, this average rate of return aggregates the returns on very different types of assets and investments: the goal is in fact to measure the average return on capital in a given society taken as a whole, ignoring differences in individual situations. ….." (Chapter Six/The Capital-Labor Split in the Twenty-First Century)

Finally, he concludes the **central contradiction of capitalism as r > g**.

Piketty's definition of capital offers nothing new and basically follows the definition prevalent in Political Economy since its classical days. This definition clings to appearances and believes them to be the ultimate. Blindly operating average, apparent data, is the 'secret' of the capitalist economy, invented to hide the intrinsic interconnections of the capital'.[14]

Capital, in the prevalent economic literature, has been generally defined as 'accumulated wealth that is traded over again', as 'accumulated or capitalized interest'. "Capital, with compound interest on every portion of capital saved, is so all engrossing that all the wealth in the world from which income is derived, has long become the interest on capital", wrote The Economist, London, way back in 1851.[15]

Since Piketty refers to Marx in this context, it is imperative to state that Marx's definition of capital and its basic contradiction evolved in course of the critique of this very Political Economy. Hence, a brief summary of Marx's position, in his own words, on all the points mentioned above by Piketty will not be out of place. This will bring out the inconsistencies in Piketty's definition as well.

Marx defined **capital as self-expanding value-form**. Social capital is social wealth exchanged (or traded) in self-expanding mode. This self-expanding value-form assumes different avatars at different stages of the development of capital.

CAPITAL AS SELF-EXPANDING VALUE-FORM

Describing the genesis of **industrial capital**, Marx writes, "The circuit M → C → M, buying in order to sell dearer, is seen most clearly in genuine merchants' capital. But the movement takes place entirely within the sphere of circulation. Since, however, it is impossible, by circulation alone to account for the conversion of money into capital, for the formation of surplus value. It would appear that merchants' capital is an impossibility **so long as equivalents are exchanged**; that, therefore, it can only have its origin in the twofold advantage gained, over both the selling and the buying producers, by the merchant who parasitically shoves himself in between them. It is in this sense that Franklin says, 'war is robbery, commerce is generally cheating.' ….Turn and twist as we may, the fact remains unaltered. **If equivalents are exchanged, no surplus value results, and if non-equivalents are exchanged, still no surplus value**. **Circulation, or the exchange of commodities, begets no value**.

The reason is now therefore plain why, in analyzing the standard form of capital, the form under which it determines the economic organization of modern society, we entirely left out of consideration its most popular, and, so to say, antediluvian forms, merchants' capital and money-lenders' capital. ….

We have shown that surplus value cannot be created by circulation, and therefore, that in its formation something must take place in the background, which is not apparent in the circulation itself. ..The commodity owner can, by his labor, create value, **but not self-expanding value**. He can increase the value of his commodity, by adding fresh labor, and therefore more value to the value in hand, by making, for instance, leather into boots. The same material has now more value, because it contains a greater quantity of labor. ..It is therefore impossible that outside the sphere of circulation, a producer of commodities can, without coming into contact with other commodity owners, expand value and consequently convert money or commodities into capital. It is therefore impossible for capital to be produced by circulation, and it is equally impossible for it to originate apart from circulation. **It must have its origin both in circulation and yet not in circulation**. We have, therefore, got a double result.

The conversion of money into capital has to be explained on the basis of the laws that regulate the exchange of commodities, in such a way that the starting point is the **exchange of equivalents**. Our friend , Moneybags, who as yet is only an embryo capitalist must buy his commodities at their value, must sell them at their value, and yet at the end of the process must withdraw more value from circulation than he threw into it at starting. His development into a full grown capitalist must take place within the sphere of circulation and without it. These are the conditions of the problem. ..

The change must, therefore, take place in the commodity bought by the first act, M → C, but not in its value, for equivalents are exchanged, and the commodity is paid for at its full value. We are, therefore, forced to the conclusion that the change originates in the use-value, as such, of the commodity, i.e., in its consumption. In order to be able to extract value from the consumption of a commodity, our friend, Moneybags, must be so lucky as to find, **within the sphere of circulation, in the market, a commodity, whose use-value possesses the peculiar property of being a source of value, whose actual consumption, therefore, is itself an embodiment of labor, and consequently, a creation of value. The possessor of money does find on the market such a special commodity in capacity for labor or labor power.**"[16]

LABOR-POWER

"The continuation of this relation demands that the owner of the labor-power should sell it only for a definite period, for if he were to sell it rump and stump, once for all, he would be selling himself, converting himself from a free man into a slave, from an owner of a commodity into a commodity. He must constantly look upon his labor-power as his own property, his own commodity, and this he can only do by placing it at the disposal of the buyer temporarily for a definite period of time. By this means alone can he avoid renouncing his rights of ownership over it. ....

The second essential condition to the owner of money finding labor-power in the market as a commodity is this – that the laborer instead of being in the position to sell commodities in which his labor is incorporated must be obliged to offer for sale as a commodity that very labor-power, which exists only in his living self. ..

For the conversion of his money into capital, therefore, the owner of money must meet in the market with free laborer, free in the double sense, that as a free man he can dispose of his labor-power as his own commodity, and that on the other hand he has no other commodity for sale, is short of everything necessary for the realization of his labor-power. ..

The value of labor-power is determined, as in case of every other commodity, by the labor-time necessary for the production, and consequently also the reproduction, of this special article. **So far it has value, it represents no more than a definite quantity of the average labor of society incorporated in it**. Labor-power exists only as a capacity, or power of the living individual. Its production consequently pre-supposes his existence. Given the individual, the production of labor-power consists in his reproduction of himself or his maintenance. For his maintenance, he requires a given quantity of the means of subsistence. Therefore the labor-time requisite for the production of labor-power reduces itself to that necessary for the production of those means of subsistence; in other words, the value of labor-power is the value of the means of subsistence necessary for the maintenance of the laborer. Labor-power, however, becomes a reality only by its exercise; it sets itself in action only by working. But thereby a definite quantity of human muscle, nerve, brain, &c., is wasted, and these require to be restored. ....The owner of labor-power is mortal. If then his appearance in the market is to be continuous, and the continuous conversion of money into capital assumes this, the seller of labor-power must perpetuate himself, 'in the way that every living individual perpetuates himself, by procreation.' The labor-power withdrawn from the market by wear and tear and death, must be continuously replaced by, at the very least, an equal amount of fresh labor-power. Hence the sum of the means of subsistence necessary for the production of labor-power must include the means necessary for the laborers' substitutes, i.e., his children, in order that this race of peculiar commodity-owners may perpetuate its appearance in the market.

In order to modify the human organism, so that it may acquire skill and handiness in a given branch of industry, and become labor-power of a special kind, a special education or training is requisite, and this, on its part, costs an equivalent in commodities of a greater or less amount. This amount varies according to the more-or-less complicated character of the labor-power. The expenses of this education (excessively small in the case of ordinary labor-power), enter pro tanto into the total value spent in its production. ....

The consumption of labor-power is at one and the same time the production of commodities and of surplus-value. The consumption of labor-power is completed as in the case of every other commodity, outside the limits of the market or of the sphere of circulation. ..Therefore, **the value of labor-power and the value which that labor-power creates in the labor-process are two entirely**

different magnitudes; and this difference of the two values was what the capitalist had in view, when he was purchasing the labor-power. What really influenced him was the specific use-value which this commodity possesses of being **a source not only of value, but of more value than it has itself.** ….

Every condition of the problem is satisfied, while the laws that regulate the exchange of commodities, have been in no way violated. Equivalent has been exchanged for equivalent. ..This metamorphosis, this conversion of money into capital, takes place both within the sphere of circulation and also outside it. ...By turning his money into commodities that serve as the material elements of a new product, and as factors in the labor-process, by incorporating living labor with their dead substance, the capitalist at the same time converts value, i.e., past materialized, and dead labor into capital, into value big with value, a live monster that is fruitful and multiplies. ..**The capitalist again and again appropriates, without equivalent, a portion of the previously materialized labor of others, and exchanges it for a greater quantity of living labor.** ..

It is the natural property of living labor, to transmit old value, whilst it creates new. Hence, with the increase in efficacy, extent and value of its means of production, consequently with the accumulation that accompanies the development of its productive power, labor keeps up and eternizes an always increasing capital-value in a form ever new. **This natural power of labor takes the appearance of an intrinsic property of capital, in which it is** incorporated; just as the productive forces of social labor take the appearance of inherent properties of capital, and as the constant appropriation of surplus-labor by the capitalists, takes that of a constant self-expansion of capital. ...."[17]

Piketty does not admit any human element in the making of capital.

ACCUMULATION OF CAPITAL

"This gratuitous service of past labor, when seized and filled with a soul by living labor increases with the advancing stages of accumulation. Past labor always disguises itself as capital. ..Capital is **not a fixed magnitude**, but is a part of social wealth, elastic and constantly fluctuating with the division of fresh surplus-value into revenue and additional capital. ..Even with a given magnitude of functioning capital, the labor-power, the science, and the land (by which are to be understood, economically, all conditions of labor furnished by Nature independently of man), embodied in it, form elastic powers of capital, allowing it, within certain limits, a field of action independent of its magnitude. ...Classical economy always loved to conceive social capital as a fixed magnitude of a fixed degree of efficiency. ...

Accumulation of wealth at one pole is, therefore, at the same time accumulation of misery, agony of toil slavery, ignorance, brutality, mental degradation, at the opposite, i.e., on the side of the class that produces its own product in the form of capital. ..

The circulation of money as capital is an end in itself, for the expansion of value takes place only within this constantly renewed movement. The circulation of capital has therefore no limits. ..As the conscious representative of this movement, the possessor of money becomes a capitalist. ..Use-values must therefore never be looked upon as the real aim of the capitalist; neither must the profit of any single transaction. **The restless, never-ending process of profit-making alone is what he aims at**. ..”[18]

Thus, according to Marx, the basic cause of capital accumulation is inherent in the very definition of capital as 'self-expanding value'. **Unpaid labor is the ultimate source**.

INTEREST-BEARING CAPITAL

What happens when capital itself is traded as a commodity? "Its use-value then consists precisely in the profit it produces. ..In this capacity of potential capital, as a means of producing profit, it becomes a commodity, but a commodity *sui generis*. Or what amounts to the same, capital as capital becomes a commodity."

"Capital manifests itself as capital through self-expansion. The degree of its self-expansion expresses the quantitative degree in which it realizes itself as capital. The surplus-value or profit produced by it – its rate or magnitude – is measurable only by comparison with the value of the advanced capital. The greater or lesser self-expansion of **interest-bearing capital** is, therefore, likewise only measurable by comparing the amount of interest, its share in the total profits, with the value of the advanced capital.

If, therefore, price expresses the value of the commodity, then interest expresses the self-expansion of money-capital and thus appears as the price paid for it to the lender. ....

Capital appears as a commodity, inasmuch as it is offered on the market, and the use-value of money is actually alienated as capital. Its use-value, however, lies in producing profit. ..The product of capital is profit. ....

Furthermore, capital appears as a commodity inasmuch as the division of profit into interest and profit proper is regulated by supply and demand, that is, by competition, just as the market-prices of commodities. ..**In any event the average rate of profit is to be regarded as the ultimate determinant of the maximum limit of interest**. ..(Here we will not go into the fluctuations in the rate of interest during the cycles in which modern industry moves – state of inactivity, mounting revival, prosperity, over-production, crisis, stagnation, state of inactivity, etc., or due to other reasons.)"[19]

"As a nation advances in the career of wealth, a class of men springs up and increases, more and more, who by the labors of their ancestors find themselves in the possession of funds sufficiently ample to afford a handsome maintenance from the interest alone. Very many also who during youth and middle age were actively engaged in business, retire in their latter days to live quietly on the interest of the sums they have themselves accumulated. This class, as well as the former, has a tendency to increase with the increasing riches of the country, for those who begin with a tolerable stock are likely to make an independence sooner than they who commence with little.

Thus it comes to pass, that in old and rich countries, the amount of national capital belonging to those who are unwilling to take the trouble of employing it themselves, bears a larger proportion to the whole productive stock of the society, than in newly settled and poorer districts. How much more numerous in proportion to the population is the class of **rentiers** ..in England! As the class of rentiers increases, so also does that of lenders of capital, for they are one and the same."[20]

"Moreover, as concerns the perpetually fluctuating market rate of interest, however, it exists at any moment as a fixed magnitude, just as the market-price of commodities, because in the money-market all **loanable capital** continually faces **functioning capital** as an aggregate mass, so that the relation between the supply of loanable capital on one side, and the demand for it on the other, decides the market level of interest at any given time. This is all the more so, the more the development, and the attendant concentration, of the credit system (ever-growing control over the money-savings of all classes of society that is effected through the bankers, and the progressive concentration of these savings in amounts which can serve as money-capital) **gives to loanable capital a general social character** and throws it all at once on the money-market. On the other hand, **the general rate of profit is never anything more than a tendency, a movement to equalize specific rates of profit**. The competition between capitalists – which is itself this movement toward equilibrium – consists here of their gradually withdrawing capital from spheres in which profit is for an appreciable length of time below average, and gradually investing capital into spheres in which profit is above average. Or it may also consist in additional capital distributing itself gradually and in varying proportions among these spheres. It is continual variation in supply and withdrawal of capital in regard to these different spheres, and never a simultaneous mass effect, as in the determination of the rate of interest. ....

In emphasizing this difference between the rate of interest and the rate of profit, we still omit the following two points, which favor consolidation of the rate of interest: i. the historical pre-existence of interest-bearing capital and the existence of a traditional general rate of interest; ii. The far greater direct influence exerted by the world-market on establishing the rate of interest, irrespective of the economic conditions of a country, as compared with its influence on the rate of profit. ..

In the money-market only lenders and borrowers face one another. The commodity has the same form – money. All specific forms of capital in accordance with its investment in particular spheres of production or circulation are here obliterated. It exists in the undifferentiated homogenous form of independent value – money. The competition of individual spheres does not affect it. They are all thrown together as borrowers of money, and capital confronts them all in a form, in which it is as yet indifferent to the prospective manner of investment. It obtains most emphatically in the supply and demand of capital as **essentially the common capital of a class** – something industrial capital does only in the movement and competition of capital between the various individual spheres. On the other hand, money-capital in the money-market actually possesses the form, in which, indifferent to its specific employment, it is divided as a common element among the various spheres, among the capitalist class, as the requirements of production in each individual spheres may dictate. Moreover, with the development of large-scale industry money-capital, so far as it appears on the market, is not represented by some individual capitalist, not the owner of one or another fraction of capital in the market, but also assumes the nature of a concentrated, organized mass, which, quite different from actual production, is subject to the control of bankers, i.e., **the representatives of social capital**. So that, **as concerns the form of demand, loanable capital is confronted by the class as a whole, whereas in the province of supply it is loanable capital which obtains *en masse*.**"[21]

"These are some of the reasons why the general rate of profit appears blurred and hazy alongside the definite interest rate, which may fluctuate in magnitude, but always confronts borrowers as given and fixed because it varies uniformly for all of them. Just as variations in the value of money do not prevent it from having the same value vis-à-vis all commodities, just as the daily fluctuations in market-prices of commodities do not prevent them from being daily reported in the papers, so the rate of interest is regularly reported as the 'price of money'. It is so, because capital itself is being offered here in the form of money as a commodity. The fixation of its price is thus a fixation of its market-price, as with all other commodities. The rate of interest, therefore, always appears as the general rate of interest, as so much money for so much money, as a definite quantity. The rate of profit, on the other hand, may vary even within the same sphere of commodities with the same price, depending on different conditions under which different capitals produce the same commodity, because the rate of profit of an individual capital is not determined by the market-price of a commodity, but rather by the difference between market-price and cost-price. And these different rates of profit can strike a balance – first within the same sphere and then between different spheres – only through continual fluctuations."[22]

"For the productive capitalist who works on borrowed capital, the gross profit falls into two parts – the interest, which he is to pay the lender, and the surplus over and above the interest, which makes up his own share of the profit. If the general rate of profit is given, this latter portion is determined by the rate of interest; and if the rate of interest is given, then by the general rate of profit.
….And, indeed, **regardless of whether the capital employed by the active capitalist is borrowed or not, and whether the capital belonging to the money-capitalist is employed by himself or not, the profit of every capital, and consequently also the average profit established by the equalization of capitals, splits, or is separated, into two qualitatively different, mutually independent and separately individualized parts, to wit – interest and profit of enterprise – both of which are determined by separate laws.** The capitalist operating on his own capital, like the one operating on borrowed capital, divides the gross profit into interest due to himself as owner, as his own lender, and into profit of enterprise due to him as to an active capitalist performing his function.

..The employer of capital, even when working with his own capital, splits into two personalities – the owner of capital and the employer of capital; with reference to the categories of profit which it yields, his capital also splits into **capital-property**, capital **outside** the production process, and yielding interest of itself, and **capital in the production process** which yields a profit of enterprise through its function. ...."[23]

MANAGERIAL AND ENTREPRENEURIAL LABOR

"Since the specific social attribute of capital under capitalist production – that of being property commanding the labor-power of another – becomes fixed, so that interest appears as a part of surplus value produced by capital in this inter-relation, the other part of surplus value – profit of enterprise – must necessarily appear as coming not from capital as such, but from the process of production, separated from its specific social attribute, whose distinct mode of existence is already expressed by the term interest on capital. But the process of production, separated from capital, is simply a labor-process. Therefore, the **industrial capitalist, as distinct from the owner of capital, does not appear as operating capital, but rather as a functionary irrespective of capital, or as a simple agent of the labor-process in general, as a laborer, and indeed as a wage laborer**.

Interest as such expresses precisely the existence of the conditions of labor as capital, in their social anti-thesis to labor, and in their transformation into personal power vis-à-vis and over labor. It represents the ownership of capital as a means of appropriating the products of the labor of others. But it represents this characteristic of capital as something which belongs to it outside the production process and by no means is the result of the specifically capitalist attribute of this production process itself. Interest represents this characteristic not as directly counter-posed to labor, but rather as unrelated to labor, and simply as a relationship of one capitalist to another; hence, as an attribute outside of, irrelevant to the relation of capital to labor. **In interest, therefore, in that specific form of profit in which the antithetical character of capital assumes an independent form, this is done in such a way that the antithesis is completely obliterated and abstracted**. Interest is a relationship between two capitalist not between capitalist and laborer.

On the other hand, this form of interest lends the other portion of profit the qualitative form of profit of enterprise, and further of **wages of superintendence**. The specific functions, which the capitalist as such has to perform, and which fall to him as distinct from and opposed to the laborer are presented as mere functions of labor. He creates surplus-value not because he works as a **capitalist**, but because he **also** works, regardless of his capacity of capitalist. This portion of surplus-value is thus no longer surplus-value, but its opposite, an equivalent for labor performed. Due to the alienated character of capital, its antithesis to labor, being relegated to a place outside the actual process of exploitation, namely to the interest-bearing capital, **this process of exploitation itself appears as a simple labor-process in which the functioning capitalist merely performs a different kind of labor than the laborer.** ....

The conception of profit of enterprise as the wages of supervising labor, arising from the antithesis of profit of enterprise to interest, is further strengthened by the fact **that a portion of profit may, indeed, be separated, and is separated in reality, as wages, or rather the reverse, that a portion of wages appears under capitalist production as integral part of profit. This portion, as Adam Smith correctly deduced, presents itself in pure form, independently and wholly separated from profit (as the sum of interest and profit of enterprise), on the one hand, and on the other, from that portion of profit which remains, after interest is deduced, as profit of enterprise in the salary of management of those branches of business whose size, etc., permits of a sufficient division of labor to justify a special salary for a manager.** ....

Stock companies in general – developed with the credit system have an increasing tendency to separate this work of management as a function from the ownership of capital, be it self-owned or borrowed. ....

Since, on the one hand, the mere owner of capital, the money-capitalist, has to face the functioning capitalist, while money-capital itself assumes a social character with the advance of credit, being concentrated in banks and loaned out of them instead of its original owners, and since, on the other hand, the mere manager who has no title whatever to the capital, whether through borrowing it or otherwise, performs all the real functions pertaining to the functioning capitalist as such, only the functionary remains and the capitalist disappears as superfluous from the production process. ….

On the basis of capitalist production a new swindle develops in stock enterprises with respect to wages of management, in that boards of numerous managers or directors are placed above the actual director, for whom supervision and management serve only as a pretext to plunder the stockholders and amass wealth."[24]

Piketty includes entrepreneurial and top managerial work in the category of labor.

FETISH CAPITAL

"The relations of capital assume their most externalized and most **fetish-like form** in interest-bearing capital. We have here $M \rightarrow M'$, money creating more money, self-expanding value, without the process that effectuates these two extremes. ….

It is a relationship of magnitudes, a relationship of the principal sum as a given value to itself as a self-expanding value, as a principal sum which has produced a surplus value. And capital as such, as we have seen, assumes this form of a directly self-expanding value for all active capitalists, whether they operate on their own or borrowed capital.

$M \rightarrow M'$. We have here the original starting point of capital, money in the formula $M \rightarrow C \rightarrow M'$ reduced to its two extremes $M \rightarrow M'$, in which $M' = M + \Delta M$, money creating more money. It is the primary and general formula of capital reduced to a meaningless condensation. ..Capital appears as a mysterious self-creating source of interest – the source of its own increase. ..**In interest-bearing capital, therefore, this automatic fetish, self-expanding value, money generating money, is brought out in their pure state and in this form it no longer bears the birthmarks of its origin**. ..**Thus we get the fetish form of capital and the conception of fetish capital**. In M $\rightarrow$ M′ we have the meaningless form of capital, the perversion and objectification of production relations in their highest degree, the interest-bearing form, the simple form of capital, in which it antecedes its own process of reproduction. It is the capacity of money, or of a commodity, to expand its own value independently of reproduction – which is a mystification of capital in its most flagrant form. **For vulgar political economy, which seeks to represent capital as an independent source of value, of value creation, this form is naturally a veritable find, a form in which the source of profit is no longer discernible, and in which the result of the capitalist process of production divorced from the process – acquires an independent existence**. ..As the growing process is to trees, so generating money appears innate in capital in its form of money-capital. ..**Money is now pregnant.** ..Interest on it grows, no matter whether it is awake or asleep, is at home or abroad, by day or by night. ..In its capacity of interest-bearing capital, capital claims the ownership of all wealth which can ever be produced, and everything it has received so far is but an installment for its all-engrossing appetite. By its innate laws, all surplus-labor which the human race can ever perform belongs to it. **Moloch**. .."[25]

The product of past labor, the past labor itself, is here pregnant in itself with a portion of present or future living surplus-value. "We know, however, that in reality **the preservation, and to that extent also the reproduction of the value of products of past labor is only the result of their contact with living labor over living surplus-labor lasts only as long as the relations of capital, which rest on those particular social relations in which past labor independently and overwhelmingly dominates over living labor**. …

The formula **capital → interest**, as third to **land → rent** and **labor → wages**, is much more consistent than **capital → profit**, **since in profit there still remains a recollection of its origin, which is not only extinguished in interest, but is also placed in a form thoroughly antithetical to this origin**. .."[26]

While unraveling inequality inherent in the very nature of social capital, **Piketty gets trapped in the conception of fetish capital** (representing capital as an independent source of value-creation). **This is the second major inconsistency of the book**. Big data methodology can lead Piketty only to this fetish of capital. In that case he can, at best, only think of **containing capital**. He desists from imagining other forms of organization or mode of production, and hides that option in brackets (Chapter One/Income and Output/The Capital-Labor Split in the Long Run: Not So Stable).

BASIC CONTRADICTION OF CAPITALISM

Piketty's formulation of the **basic contradiction of capitalism** as **r** (rate of return on capital) > **g** (rate of growth) is a natural corollary to his capital fetishism. This matter of fact statement (supported by data spread over two centuries) hardly guides us to explore the inner world of capitalist production, and offers nothing new by way of propositions and explanations.

For Marx, "The **real barrier** of capitalist production is **capital itself**. It is that capital and its self-expansion appear as the starting and the closing point, the motive and purpose of production; that production is only production for **capital** and not vice-versa, the means of production are not mere means for a constant expansion of the living process of the **society of producers**. The limits within which the preservation and self-expansion of the value of capital resting on the expropriation and pauperization of the great mass of producers can alone move – these limits come continually into conflict with the methods of production employed by capital for its purposes, which drive towards unlimited extension of production, towards production as an end in itself, towards unconditional development of the social productivity of labor. **The means – unconditional development of the productive forces of society – comes continually into conflict with the limited purpose, the self-expansion of the existing capital**.
..Things are produced only so long as they can be produced with a profit .. having an eye solely for the development of the productive forces, **whatever the cost in human beings and capital-values**."[27]

WITH ADEQUATE PROFIT, CAPITAL IS VERY BOLD. A CERTAIN 10% WILL ENSURE ITS EMPLOYMENT ANYWHERE; 20% CERTAIN WILL PRODUCE EAGERNESS; 50%, POSITIVE AUDACITY; 100% WILL MAKE IT READY TO TRAMPLE ON ALL HUMAN LAWS; 300%, AND THERE IS NOT A CRIME AT WHICH IT WILL SCRUPLE, NOR A RISK IT WILL NOT RUN, EVEN TO THE CHANCE OF ITS OWNER BEING HANGED. IF TURBULENCE AND STRIFE WILL BRING A PROFIT, IT WILL FREELY ENCOURAGE BOTH. SMUGGLING AND THE SLAVE TRADE HAVE AMPLY PROVED, ALL THAT IS HERE STATED. T J Dunning (1799-1873), "Trades' Unions and Strikes: Their Philosophy and Intention", London, 1860.[28]

"The growing discordance between the productive development of society and the relations of production hitherto characteristic of it, is expressed in acute contradictions, crises, convulsions. The violent destruction of capital as the condition for its self-preservation, and not because of external circumstances, is the most striking form in which it is ADVISED TO BE GONE AND TO GIVE ROOM TO A HIGHER STATE OF SOCIAL PRODUCTION. ...

THESE CONTRADICTIONS LEAD TO EXPLOSIONS, CATACLYSMS, CRISES, IN WHICH BY MOMENTANEOUS SUSPENSION OF LABOR AND ANNIHILATION OF A GREAT PORTION OF CAPITAL THE LATTER IS VIOLENTLY REDUCED TO THE POINT WHERE IT CAN GO ON FULLY EMPLOYING ITS PRODUCTIVE POWERS WITHOUT COMMITTING SUICIDE. YET, THESE REGULARLY RECURRING CATASTROPHES LEAD TO THEIR REPETITION ON A HIGHER SCALE, AND FINALLY TO ITS VIOLENT OVERTHROW."[29]

Mr Piketty can here well remember the period 1914 - 1950.

CAPITAL ETERNAL AND TRANSIENT

TRUE WEALTH …. [IS] THE COMPLETE ENJOYMENT NOT ONLY OF THE NECESSITIES OF LIFE BUT ALSO OF ALL THE SUPERFLUITIES AND OF ALL THAT CAN GIVE PLEASURE TO THE SENSES. .. THESE METALS (GOLD AND SILVER) HAVE BEEN TURNED INTO AN **IDOL**, AND DISREGARDING THE GOAL AND PURPOSE THEY WERE INTENDED TO FULFIL IN COMMERCE, i.e. TO SERVE AS PLEDGE IN EXCHANGE AND RECIPROCAL TRANSFER, THEY WERE ALLOWED TO ABANDON THIS SERVICE ALMOST ENTIRELY IN ORDER TO BE TRANSFORMED INTO **DIVINITIES** TO WHOM MORE GOODS, VALUABLES AND EVEN **HUMAN BEINGS** WERE SACRIFICED AND CONTINUE TO BE SACRIFICED, THAN WERE EVER SACRIFICED TO THE FALSE DIVINITIES IN BLIND ANTIQUITY WHICH FOR SO LONG WERE THE WHOLE CULT AND THE WHOLE RELIGION FOR MOST PEOPLES. THUS THE SLAVE OF COMMERCE HAS BECOME ITS MASTER. .. MONEY .. HAS BECOME THE EXECUTIONER OF ALL THINGS. .. MONEY .. DECLARES WAR .. ON THE WHOLE HUMAN RACE.

BOISGUILLEBERT.[30]

In Piketty's definition of capital everything is included – from Upper Palaeolithic and Mesolithic caves, tents, huts, to land in Middle Ages, to smart phones of our time. He writes, "Historically, the earliest forms of capital accumulation involved both tools and improvements to land (fencing, irrigation, drainage, etc.) and rudimentary dwellings (caves, tents, huts, etc.). Increasingly sophisticated forms of industrial and business capital came later, as did constantly improved forms of housing." (Chapter Six/What is Capital Used For?)

Thus, so far as human society is concerned, capital is presented as an **eternal** category, permanently embedded in all civilizations/societies. To strip this **divine** category off its divinity and to reduce it to its **historicity**, to make an **eternal** element a **transient** one, is tantamount to blasphemy in the eyes of 'pure' (in Marx's term 'vulgar') economists. And for this blasphemy, they never forgave Karl Marx. (By the way, anarchists too regard money/capital as a category immanent in all civilizations – the only difference is that while the vulgar economists view it as an underlying positive force propelling human society from one stage to another, the anarchists term this force as 'satanic' responsible for the fall of humankind. Both refuse to assign it its historicity, to characterize it as a mode of production arising at a certain stage of historical development, and hence liable to be superseded by other mode of production due to the same historical movement.)

However, when you deny divinity or eternity to capital, then, for these pure economists, the entire edifice of human society will come crashing down – hence they describe Marx's propositions as **apocalyptic**.

THE THEORY OF MARGINAL UTILITY

But this view of capital, this mixing of use-value and exchange-value, of wealth and capital is nothing new. Its origin can be traced back to the early years of classical political economy, and in case of France, especially to the writings of **Etiênne Bonnet de Condillac** (1715-1780). Condillac's 'Le Commerce et la Gouvernement' and **Adam Smith**'s 'Wealth of Nations' were published in the same year (1776), and some economists still believe that due to the paramount influence of England in the first half of the nineteenth century, Condillac's work and fame was eclipsed by Adam Smith and his 'Wealth of Nations'.

According to Condillac's theory of value, "The value of a thing consists solely **in its relation to our wants**. What is more to the one is less to the other, and vice versa. .. It is not to be assumed that we offer for sale articles required for our own consumption. .. We wish to part with a useless thing, in order to get one that we need; we want to give less for more. .. It was natural to think that, in an exchange, value was given for value, whenever each of the articles exchanged was of equal value with the same quantity of gold. .. But there is another point to be considered in our calculation. The question is, whether we both exchange something superfluous for something necessary."[31] On this Marx remarks, "We see in this passage, how Condillac not only confuses use-value with exchange-value, but in a really childish manner assumes, that in a society, in which the production of commodities is well developed, each producer produces his own means of subsistence, and throws into circulation only the excess over his own requirements. Still, Condillac's argument is frequently used by modern economists, more especially when the point is to show, that the exchange of commodities in its developed form, commerce, is productive of surplus-value."[32]

Condillac's utility theory (making use-value the basis of exchange) was in opposition to the **labor theory of value** (with all its limitations, confusions and contradictions) then propounded by leading figures of classical political economy at that time. In opposition to mercantilists, these prime movers of classical political economy shifted their attention from the **sphere of circulation** to the **sphere of production** and put forward their versions of labor theory. We may have a quick look at this stream of classical political economy:

Benjamin Franklin (1706-1790), 'scholar of American Enlightenment was among the first supporters of the labor theory of value. He for the first time deliberately and clearly (so clearly as to be almost trite) reduces exchange value to labor time.' **Boisguillebert** (1646-1714), founder of classical political economy in France, 'can be included among these figures (although he may not be aware of the implications of his observations in this respect). He reduces the exchange value of commodities to labor time, by determining the true value according to the correct proportion in which the labor time of individual producers is divided between the different branches of industry, and declaring that free competition is the social process by which this correct proportion is established.'[33]

Adam Smith: 'Labor .. is the real measure of the exchangeable value of all commodities.' ('Wealth of Nations', Book I, Chapter V)

Sismondi (1773-1842): 'A profit is made not because the industry produces much more than it costs, but because it fails to give to the workmen sufficient compensation for his toil. Such an industry is a social evil.' ('Nouveaux Principle', Volume I)

Marx's theory of surplus value evolved in course of the critique of these prevalent theories of labor value.

In the last third of the nineteenth century, Condillac's theory was resurrected in the **Theory of Marginal Utility** expounded in the works of **William Jevons** (Britain), **Léon Walras** (Switzerland), **Carl Menger**, **Friederich von Wiser** and **Eugen Böhm-Bawerk** (Austria). According to this **Austrian School of Economics**, the value of anything is deduced from its 'marginal utility', i.e. the utility of the last unit that satisfies the least important requirement of the subject – thus, exchange is based not on the exchange value, but on use-value, to which is ascribed the ability to directly correlate benefits. Their analysis centered on use-value or utility, and its subjective-psychological interpretation. Later, this school split into two camps – the **cardinalists** (**Alfred Marshall** in Britain being the most prominent representative who argued that it was possible to calibrate the absolute magnitude of marginal utility) and the **ordinalists** (**Paul Samuelson** in the USA and **John Hicks** in Britain, who considered that impossible and therefore preferred using the method of ordinary collation of preferences). The 'marginal utility' advocates deny social labor time as the determinant of value, replace labor theory of value by their subjective marginal utility theory, conceal the source of surplus value (unpaid labor of workers), and thus disguise the exploitation of labor by capital.

THE THEORY OF MARGINAL PRODUCTIVITY

Side by side with this theory of marginal utility, there arose the theory of marginal productivity around the same time (late 19th century) elaborated by the American economist **John Bates Clark** (1847-1938). According to this theory, the source of value is the productivity of the 'production factors' (labor, capital and land). Each production factor is involved in the process of production and is therefore productive. Each factor of production participates in creating a product's value to the extent of its marginal productivity, i.e. the amount of the 'marginal product' it creates. The 'marginal product' is the increase in output resulting from increasing this production factor by one unit, with all the factors being unchanged. According to this theory, the 'marginal product' determines the 'fair' incomes paid to each of the factors. Thus the 'marginal product' of capital is interest. The workers' wages are determined by the 'marginal product of labor'. An increase in the number of people working at an enterprise tends to reduce the productivity of labor of each newly employed worker, given the unchanged amount of capital and same technical level. The entrepreneur stops employing workers when a worker is unable to produce the amount of commodities needed to provide for his existence. The productivity of this particular worker is 'marginal productivity', and the marginal product he produces is 'natural', or 'fair', payment for his work. Thus, the amount of one's wages is made dependent on productivity and employment levels. The more the workers are employed, the lower the productivity and the lower the wages. According to this reasoning, unemployment is caused by workers' demanding wages which exceed the 'marginal product'. Thus, wages are taken out of the context of social and class relationships and are divorced from capitalist relations of production, those of exploitation of labor by capital. They are presented as the 'natural' price of labor, as a non-historical category.

RETURN ON CAPITAL

On the question of rate of return on capital, Piketty knows that "the very notion of an 'average' rate of return on capital is a fairly abstract concept. In practice the rate of return varies widely with the type of asset, as well as with the size of individual fortunes. The capital shares and average rates of return were calculated by adding the various amounts of income from capital included in national accounts, regardless of legal classifications (rents, profits, dividends, interest, royalties, etc., excluding interest on public debt and before taxes) and then dividing this total by national income (which gives the share of capital income in national income, denoted by α) or by the national capital stock (which gives the average rate of return on capital, denoted r). By construction, this average rate of return aggregates the returns on very different types of assets and investments: the goal is in fact to measure the average return on capital in a given society taken as a whole, ignoring differences in individual situations." (Chapter Six/The Capital-Labor Split in the Twenty-First Century)

He further accepts that "**in any event, it is important to point out that no self-corrective mechanism exists to prevent a steady increase of the capital/income ratio, β, together with a steady rise in capital's share of national income, α**."

Moreover, he is quite aware that '**pure return earned by the largest fortunes are significantly higher than the levels indicated here**'; and '**it is likely that such high returns also include a non-negligible portion of**

remuneration for informal entrepreneurial labor.'
(Chapter Six/The Notion of the Pure Return on Capital)

Criticizing Marx's concept of the 'falling rate of profit' (on this subject I will come back later) and providing a summary of the controversies during 1950s and 1960s between Robert Solow and Paul Samuelson (based primarily in Cambridge, Massachusetts) on the one hand, and **Joan Robinson**, **Nicholas Kaldor** and **Luigi Pasinetti** (based in Cambridge, England) on the other hand, Piketty reveals his own **theoretical foundation** guiding his data mining and processing. (Chapter Six/Beyond the Two Cambridges/What is Capital Used For)

Piketty further explains, "In any case, the rate of return on capital is determined by the following two forces: first technology (what is capital used for?), and second, the abundance of the capital stock (too much capital kills the return on capital). .. It is natural to expect that the **marginal productivity of capital** decreases as the stock of capital increases. In particular, the central question is how much the return on capital r decreases (assuming that it is equal to the **marginal productivity of capital**) when the capital/income ratio β increases. Two cases are possible. If the return on capital r falls more than proportionately when the capital/income ratio β increases (for example, if r decreases by more than half when β is doubled), then the share of capital income in national income $\alpha = r \times \beta$ decreases when β increases. In other words, the decrease in the return on capital more than compensates for the increase in the capital/income ratio. Conversely, if the return r falls less than proportionately when β increases (for example, if r decreases by less than half when β is doubled), then capital's share α = r x β increases when β increases. In that case, **the effect of the decreased return on capital is simply to cushion and moderate the increase in the capital share compared to the increase in the capital/income ratio.**" (We will later see how Marx explains this phenomenon in his theory of the 'tendency of the average rate of profit to decline'.

NEO-KEYNESIANISM AND CONCEPT OF PRODUCTION FUNCTION

Here, it will not be out of place to mention that in the 1950s the British economist **Roy Harrod** and the America economist **Evsey Domar** developed a neo-Keynesian theory of economic growth. Actually, for almost four decades (from 1930s to 1970s), Keynesians of different schools ruled the economic scene – i. **Alvin Hansen, John Hicks, Stuart Chase**, Paul Samuelson (neo-Keynesian theory of the cyclical development of the capitalist economy). They maintained that the public sector has lost its capitalist nature, and due to the revolution in the functions of a bourgeois state in the 20th century, state economic and social measures can eliminate any contradictory developments and ensure crisis-free progress, and stable and high growth rates; ii. **Paul Davidson, Robert Clower, Alex Leijonhufvud**: they emphasized on restoring the monetary aspects of Keynesianism in order to adapt them to the analysis and regulation of inflationary situations; iii. Joan Robinson, **Piero Sraffa** and Luigi Pasinetti: they were left and radical interpreters of Keynes; iv. Roy Harrod and Evsey Domar (neo-Keynesian theory of economic growth): models created by them emphasized on the rate of accumulation as a principal strategic factor and a basic parameter for regulating long-term growth. The growth rate is stable if the share of savings in the income and the capital co-efficient are also stable (the so-called guaranteed growth rate). However, they cautioned that this stability is not maintained automatically. Deviations of actual growth rates from the guaranteed rates engender cyclic vacillations. To maintain stable growth, the state has to interfere and make it sure that demand is effective.

American economist Robert Solow improved upon the Domar-Harrod theory of economic growth and provided an upgraded neo-classical growth model – in 1956 he introduced the concept of **'production function'** with substitutable factors and inverted Domar's formula ($g = s/\beta$) and wrote $\beta = s/g$. According to him, in the long run, the capital/income ratio adjusts to the savings rate and structural growth rate of the economy rather than the other way round. (Robinson, Kaldor and Pasinetti 'saw in Solow's model a claim that growth is always perfectly balanced, thus negating the importance Keynes had attached to short-term fluctuations. ..) **'It was not until 1970s that Solow's so-called neo-classical growth model definitively carried the day.'** (Piketty/Beyond the Two Cambridges)

The world economic crisis of 1974-75 (stagflation) signaled the decline of Keynesianism, giving way to the rise of supply-side monetarist Chicago School of economists led by Milton Friedman. After the Thatcherite reforms in Britain (1979) and advent of Reaganonomics in the United States (1980), this Chicago School dominated the economic scene for the next (almost) three decades (since 1980s).

PIKETTY'S NOTE OF CAUTION

Piketty has seen all this and, therefore, he sounds a note of caution, "In fact, the stability of capital's share of income – assuming it turns out to be true – **in no way guarantees harmony; it is compatible with extreme and untenable inequality of the ownership of capital and distribution of income**. Contrary to a widespread idea, moreover, stability of capital's share of national income in no way implies stability of capital/income ratio, **which can easily take on very different values at different times and in different countries, so that, in particular, there can be substantial international imbalances in the ownership of capital**. The point I want to emphasize, however, is that historical reality is more complex than the idea of a completely stable capital-labor split suggests. ..**From 1990s on, however, numerous studies mention a significant increase in the share of national income in rich countries going to profits and capital after 1970, along with the concomitant decrease in the share going to wages and labor**. ..The only thing appears to be relatively well-established is that the tendency for the capital/income ratio β to rise, as has been observed in the rich countries in recent decades and might spread to other countries around the world if growth (and especially demographic growth) slows in the twenty-first century, may well be accompanied by a durable increase in capital's share of national income α. To be sure, it is likely that the return on capital, r, will decrease as β increases. But on the basis of historical experience, **the most likely outcome is that the volume effect will outweigh the price effect, which means that accumulation effect will outweigh the decrease in the return on capital**. .. Share going to capital overall continued to increase between 1990 and 2010 despite the stabilization of the profit share. .. (Chapter Six/from various sections)

PIKETTY'S THEORETICAL MODEL

Despite notes of caution and matter-of-fact statements, if one goes through Piketty's analyses and explanations, his theoretical lineage can well be detected. His data points to other direction (towards Marx); he is aware that various supply-side and demand-side prescriptions to realize somewhat stable and balanced growth of capitalist economy have been futile, and at best, have only short-term effects; he accepts that no self-corrective mechanism exists to prevent a steady increase of the capital/income ratio, together with a steady rise in capital's share of national income; yet, he clings to the theory of marginal utility and productivity **that masks the social relationships and contradictions inherent in capital**. Taking recourse to aggregate data too helps in this task. Piketty revives, in a somewhat modified form, a particular strand of neo-Keynesianism in the background of the Great Recession of 2008-09, and widespread resentment and protests against the neo-liberal free market policies that have been ruling the economic scene for the last three decades. Although opposed to free market fundamentalism, he does not oppose neo-liberal market reforms and strives to marry opening of the markets with neo-Keynesian state interventions in order not to strike a harmony (he knows such an attempt would be impractical), but to contain the free run of capitalist accumulation as well as to strengthen the forces of **convergence.** He is very much disappointed on the score of raising the growth rate, and hence, apart from his 'utopian' proposal of global progressive tax on capital, he emphasizes on '**diffusion of knowledge**'. He writes, "To sum up, historical experience suggests that the principal mechanism for convergence at the international as well as the domestic level is the diffusion of knowledge. In other words, the poor catch up with the rich to the extent that they achieve the same level of technological know-how, skill, and education, not by becoming the property of the wealthy. The diffusion of knowledge is not like manna from heaven: it is often hastened by international openness and trade (autarky does not encourage technological transfer). Above all, knowledge diffusion depends on a country's ability to mobilize financing as well as institutions that encourage large-scale investment in education and training of the population while guaranteeing a stable legal framework that various economic actors can reliably count on. It is therefore closely associated with the achievement of legitimate and efficient government. Concisely stated, these are the main lessons that history has to teach about global growth and international inequalities."

On this, the less said the better. Piketty conveniently puts the entire question of distributive justice under the carpet. Historical experience and the data provided by him of the last two centuries tell the opposite story – diffusion of knowledge over the past two centuries in Europe and

America has **not** reduced inequalities within those countries as well as international inequalities. (One need not mention that basic necessities of life, living standards, etc. are relative categories. Rise in living standards of the working masses does not necessarily mean reduction in inequality. Instead, it may also mean rise in inequality, if wage rise is accompanied with faster rise in income from capital.)

His subjective-psychological theoretical foundation of marginal utility and productivity can lead him up to this level only, and put him in stark opposition to his data. **His objective data clashes with his subjective theoretical conviction**.

Piketty's theoretical genealogy may be summed up as follows: **Piketty → Robert Solow → Domar-Harrod → Paul Samuelson → J B Clark-Austrian School → Condillac.** He camouflages reality under occasional anti-capital radical rhetoric, while pursuing a subjective theoretical strand of 'pure' economics. **The theory behind his big data methodology is thus revealed, and the theory is found to be miserably incapable of incorporating in its fold the full implications of data disclosures. Data defeats Piketty's theoretical model. This is the third major inconsistency of the book.** (It is altogether another matter that if we follow alternative line of reasoning and theoretical model, we need fresh set of data and Piketty's data will prove to be very much wanting.)

CAPITAL'S CONTRADICTIONS

Aggregate return on capital (that too over a very long period of time) may be useful for accounting purposes and for general studies, it very much masks the social relationships and interconnections of capital. Hence a little elaboration on this matter will not be out of place.

Capital always exists as many capitals spread over different spheres and different countries giving different returns in the form of profit, interest, dividends, rents, royalties, etc. These capitals are always engaged in conflicts and co-ordinations among themselves. Due to uneven development of different economies/countries, and cross-border flow of capital, capital naturally flows to those sectors and countries where return is relatively high. Since the source of capital's self-expansion is unpaid labor-time, capital is bound up with the laboring classes. Wages vary in different countries and in different spheres of economy. Labor-power and raw materials are cheap in under-developed and developing countries, and exploitation of cheap labor power and raw materials provides developed capitalist economies super profits. Many of these countries were part of the primitive accumulation of capital under the colonial system, and are still functioning as that source in different forms. Due to discriminatory wages, female work force and child labor generate extra profit for capital under horrible working conditions. Much of women's productive work still remains unreported or under-reported. Similarly, there are a number of oppressed and depressed communities all over the world who were earlier traded as slaves or worked as serfs, and are still serving as a source of cheap labor – they are also victim of all sorts of racial and caste discriminations. And apart from all these, swindling, scams, tax evasions, theft, etc., continue to be the sources of capital accumulation.

Once we decompose aggregate return on capital, a whole world of inequalities comes out into the open. Data did not discover inequality. Inequality in its different dimensions has been the subject of study since the classical times. Inequality and exploitation have always been a well-known fact of life ('a naked fact', as Piketty himself mentions). For formulation of policies and programs, both ruling capitalist class and the oppressed working masses need such serious studies from time to time. Their importance cannot be underestimated.

Despite limited resources at their hands, some pioneering surveys and studies regarding horrible working conditions of male, female and child workers in different sectors of industrial economy were made in the very first half of the nineteenth century itself.

- In 1815, while traveling in England, economist **J B Say** (1767-1832) declared that a worker with a family, despite efforts often of an heroic character, could not gain more than three quarters and sometimes only a half of what was needed for his upkeep.
- In 1819, in the wake of speeches and publications of **Robert Owen** (1771-1857), an Act of Parliament was passed in the United Kingdom limiting the hours of work of children in cotton factories. "Robert Owen, soon after 1810, not only maintained the necessity of a limitation of the working-day in theory, but actually introduced the 10 hours' day into his factory at New Lanark. This was laughed at as a communist Utopia; so

were his 'Combination of children's education with productive labor' and the Co-operative Societies of workingmen, first called into being by him. To-day, the first Utopia is a Factory Act, the second figures as an official phrase in all Factory Acts, the third is already being used as a cloak for reactionary humbug."[34]

- In 1835, **Andrew Ure** ('Philosophy of Manufactures') reckoned that in the manufacture of cotton, wool, linen, and silk in England there were employed 4,800 boys and 5,308 girls below 11 years of age, 67,000 boys and 89,000 girls between 11 and 18 years of age, and 88,000 men and 1,02,000 women above 18 years.

- In 1840, in France, the great work of **Dr Villermé** (Piketty mentions his work) provided a complete description of the heart-rending life of the workers and martyrdom of their children. '**In some establishments of Normandy, the thong used for the punishment of children in the spinner's trade appears as an instrument of production.**'

- In 1845, **Frederich Engels** (1820-1895) published his 'Die Lage der arbeitenden Klasse in England' (Leipzig, 'The Condition of the Working-Class in England'). In 1842, he settled in Manchester, the center of British industry, and entered the service of a commercial firm of which his father was a shareholder. 'Here he wandered about the slums in which the workers were cooped up, and saw their poverty and misery with his own eyes. Apart from his personal observations, he read all that had been revealed before him on the condition of the British working class and carefully studied all the official documents he could get.' This book was the result of these studies and observations. 'How completely Engels understood the nature of the capitalist mode of production is shown by the Factory Reports, Reports on Mines, &c., that have appeared since 1845, and how wonderfully he painted the circumstances in detail is seen on the most superficial comparisons of his work with the official reports of the Children's Employment Commission, published 18 to 20 years later (1863-1867). Here, then, little or no alteration had been enforced, by authority, in the conditions painted by Engels. I borrow my examples chiefly from the Free-trade period after 1848, that age of paradise, of which the commercial travelers for the great firm of Free-trade, blatant as ignorant, tell such fabulous tales. ..[35]

Contradictions inherent in this social relationship (i.e. capital) began to manifest in the early stage of capitalist development. Here is a summary of these manifestations, mainly from French and European history (supplemented with Marx's brief observations).

CONTRADICTION AMONG CAPITALS

This contradiction often led to trade wars and national/colonial wars throughout the eighteenth and nineteenth centuries, and to two world wars, and a host of local wars in the twentieth century. (Twenty-First Century is no exception in this regard.) One can collect the data on these wars and can calculate the immense loss of human lives and capital-values.

About a decade after the French Revolution (1789-1794), **Napoleon I** proclaimed in 1806 the **Continental System** and forbade the countries of the continental Europe to trade with Great Britain. The countries that participated in the Continental System were Spain, the Kingdom of Naples, The Netherlands, Prussia, Denmark, Russia, Austria and others. In retaliation, through a number of royal decrees of 1807, Britain ordered neutral countries to cease all trade with France and the states that joined the Continental System in order to strengthen the naval blockade of France and to deprive her of access to colonial goods.

Since then up to the current Doha round of the WTO negotiations, one can find a series of trade conflicts and co-ordinations, protectionism, sanctions and commercial wars during the last three centuries. Even a brief description of the series of wars – local, national and world wars – is out of question in this critique.

CONTRADICTION BETWEEN CAPITAL AND LABOR

This contradiction too manifested itself in the initial years of the French Revolution. "During the very first storms of the revolution, the French bourgeoisie dare to take away from the workers the right of association but just acquired. By a decree of June 14, 1791, they declared all coalition of the workers as 'an attempt against liberty and the declaration of the rights of man', punishable by a fine of 500 livres, together with deprivation of the rights of an active citizen for one year."[36] The July Revolution of 1830 was followed by workers' insurrection in Lyons (1831), and the February 1848 Revolution by the June insurrection of workers. And it was the Paris workers' revolution of

September 4, 1870 that led to the collapse of the Second Empire of Napoleon III like a house of cards and the republic was again proclaimed (the Paris Commune, 4 September, 1870 to 28 May, 1871). In the wake of the declaration of the Paris Commune, workers in Lyons, Marseilles and Toulouse staged revolutionary armed uprisings and set up communes in their respective cities.

Workers became a formidable political force in various European countries in the second half of nineteenth century under the leadership of various Social-Democratic and Socialist Parties. Here we cannot go into that history.

Six years before the outbreak of the world economic crisis of 1974-75 (and almost three years before the birth of Thomas Piketty), Paris students and workers revolted against the **Keynesian economy of the post-war years**, what they termed as bureaucrat capitalism. Actually the **'Occupy movement'** owes its origin to this very Paris student revolt of May, 1968. It had a very modest beginning on March 22, 1968, when, following the arrest of six militants of the National Vietnam Committee, a crowd of students assembled quite spontaneously for a protest at **Nanterre** and decided to 'occupy' the administrative building. The movement that began with around 142 students only, soon swept across different cities of France and joined by hundred thousands of students and workers. **Sorbonne** was occupied, and on 14 May, workers occupied the **Sud-Aviation Works** in **Nantes**. This Occupy Movement spread rapidly and spontaneously – a host of other factories fell to the workers.[37]

A few years after the Great Recession of 2008-09, this occupy movement resurfaced in the United States, this time not against the Keynesian economy but against the neo-liberal supply-side economy.

No need to say that all these workers' movements were suppressed brutally and drowned in blood claiming the lives of hundred thousands of workers.

CONTRADICTION BETWEEN CAPITAL AND THE 'SECOND SEX'

This contradiction surfaced just after the 'Declaration of the Rights of Man and the Citizen (1789)' during the French Revolution. It is well-known that **Mary Wollstonecraft** (1759-1797) wrote his classic 'A Vindication of the Rights of Woman' (1792) in response to **Charles Maurice de Talleyrand-Périgord**'s 1791 report to the French National Assembly which stated that women should only receive a domestic education. Wollstonecraft forcefully asserted that women were not naturally inferior to men, that they should be treated as rational beings, and that men-woman equality can be realized only in a social order founded on reason.

In a letter to **Kugelmann** (December 12, 1868), Marx wrote, "Very great progress was demonstrated at the last Congress of the American Labor Union, inter alia, by the fact that it treated the women workers with full parity; by contrast, the English and to an even greater extent the gallant French, are displaying a marked narrowness of spirit in this respect. Everyone who knows anything of history also knows that **great social revolutions are** impossible without the feminine ferment. **Social progress may be measured precisely by the social position of the fair sex (plain ones included).** Ms **Harriet Law** (1832-1897), a leading figure in the atheist movement in England, was the first woman member of the General Council of the International Working Men's Association (from June 1867 to 1872). She was also the member of the Manchester Section of the International (1872).[38]

Here, of course, there is no scope to go into the history of women's movement during the last two centuries which has now (from the question of working hours, wage discrimination, voting rights, etc.) penetrated into all aspects of our life.

CONTRADICTION BETWEEN CAPITAL AND OPPRESSED NATIONS AND COMMUNITIES

By the time of the French Revolution, France was already a pre-eminent colonial power along with Britain and Holland. These colonial capitalist powers indulged in a flourishing slave trade. At the time of 'Declaration of the Rights of Man and Citizen', there were in the English West Indies ten slaves for one free man, in the French fourteen for one, in the Dutch twenty-three for one.[39] No wonder, the nascent revolutionary French Republic had to, first of all, face a formidable **slave as well as national revolt in Haiti** (earlier the French colony of Saint Domingue). The rebellion began with a revolt of African slaves in April 1791 and ended in November 1803 with the French defeat at the battle of Vertières. **The Haitian Revolution (1791-1804)** was the only slave revolt which led to the founding of a state – Haiti became an independent Republic on January 1, 1804. This revolt also culminated in the elimination of slavery – on February 4, 1794, the French Convention, in the background of this revolt, under the leadership of **Maximilien Robespierre** voted for the abolition of slavery.

Many western economists (Piketty including) still very much undermine the role of loot and plunder of colonial wealth in the making of capital.

Marx hailed the 1857 revolt in India as the 'First War of Independence', and on the Irish question, he, in a letter to **Meyer** and **Vogt** (April 9, 1870), wrote, "It is the task of the 'International' to bring the conflict between England and Ireland to the forefront everywhere, and to side with Ireland publicly everywhere. The special task of the Central Council in London is to awaken the consciousness of the English working class that, **for them, the national emancipation of Ireland is not a question of abstract justice or humanitarian sentiment, but the first condition of their own social emancipation.**"[40]

PERIODIC CYCLE OF CRISIS

Contradiction between socialized capital and privatized profit: As we have already seen, accumulation of capital has been marked by periodic cycle of crisis claiming heavy cost in human beings and capital values. Piketty avoided delving into the history of the periodic cycle of crisis – although data on this score would have provided him with greater insight into the working and movement of capitalist economy.

The periodic cycle of crisis too began in the early decades of the 19th century, just after the end of the Napoleonic Wars and restoration of the Bourbons in France. In 1815, the first crisis shook the English market, throwing a number of workers on to the street and resulting in riots and machine-breaking. During the war period, the English manufacturers were forced to accumulate the stocks which they could not export, so that on the return of peace their supplies far exceeded the demands of the Continent. In 1818, a new commercial panic, followed by fresh riots, again paralyzed the English market. But the more serious crisis of 1825 was caused by the extensive credit given to the newly opened markets of South America, led to the failure of about 70 English provincial banks, bringing much ruin in its train, as well as a shock to several neighboring countries. Since then, during the whole of 19th, 20th and to the early decade of our own 21st century, similar phenomena have recurred with striking regularity, involving ruin to ever-widening areas – world crisis of 1857, Great Depression of 1929, world economic crisis (stagflation) of 1974-75, Great Recession of 2008-09 being some of the well-known milestones.

Regarding the growth of productivity, Marx, analyzing the commercial cycle of 1837 to 1847, and of 1847 to 1857, summed up his observations as follows (Mr Piketty should note): "The law is this – that if, by over-production and over-speculation, a crisis has been brought about, still the productive powers of the nation and the faculty of absorption on the market of the world, have, in the meantime, so much expanded, that they will only temporarily recede from the highest point reached, and that after some oscillations spreading over some years, **the scale of production which marked the highest point of prosperity in one period of the commercial cycle, becomes the starting point of the subsequent period**. ..,,[41]

Further, regarding pauperism during the decennial epoch of 1849-1858, Marx observes, "The stationary million of English paupers is diminished only by 26,233 individuals. If we compare the years 1853, it has even increased by 109,364. **There must be something rotten in the very core of a social system which increases its wealth without diminishing its misery**. .."[42]

THEFT AND FRAUD

Property is not theft, but theft, fraud, scams, etc. have always been part of capital accumulation. Again we can go into the history of fraud in France itself.

In 1716, a Scottish economist and financier **John Law** founded a private bank with the backing of French ruling circles, which was turned into a state bank. In 1720, Law was appointed Controller General of Finance. He withdrew metallic money from circulation and supported various speculative undertakings such as the opening of shady trading companies, the issue of fictitious shares, etc. All these activities finally culminated, at the end of 1720, in the final collapse of the bank and 'Law's system'.

In 1852, the **Péreire brothers** founded a joint-stock bank, **'Société générale du Crédit mobilier'**. It was notorious for its speculation. Closely linked with and enjoying the protection of Napoleon III's government, the Crédit mobilier took an active part in building railways and setting up industrial enterprises. It went bankrupt in 1867.[43]

From Law's bank in the 18th century to Crédit mobilier in the 19th century to **Lehman Brothers** and **Rajat Gupta's insider trading** – fraud has been an integral part of capital all over the world during the last three centuries.

Above description (although very, very brief), I hope, brings out the social relationships bound up with capital, contradictions inherent in these relationships, and general features of capital accumulation, along with Marx's brief observations on these points. Needless to say that this line of reasoning necessitates different set of data.

All these contradictions and features of capitalist economy, in different forms are still in operation – capitalist mode of production is incapable of resolving them. One can see some improvements; but, apart from technological factors and demands of capital accumulation itself, the main reason behind these improvements lies in popular movements and revolutions - in workers', women's and oppressed masses'/communities' innumerable movements, communist/socialist revolutions, national liberation movements and popular insurrections all over the world during the last two centuries.

However, in times of crisis, the ruling classes still try to snatch or curb the democratic rights and entitlements that the working masses have earned through protracted struggles and immense sacrifices. It has well been witnessed during recent popular movements and agitations.

These improvements, as we have noted earlier, do not necessarily signify decrease in inequality. Granting short-term fluctuations and regional specificities, they may as well indicate rise in inequality. Piketty's data confirms this.

Before moving to the next topic, two things need to be clarified. During the period 1870-1900, due to the rise in wages, Piketty sees a comparable decrease in capital's share. He misses following points:

i.   It was the heyday of colonialism. Partition of Africa was finalized in the **Berlin Conference of 1884**. Except Abyssinia (Ethiopia) and Liberia, entire Africa was divided among colonial European powers.

ii.   It was also the period of **second industrial revolution**. Here, one example will be sufficient. Before the introduction of the Bessemer process, which makes steel from molten pig iron, there were hundreds of blast furnaces in the US. None produced more than 1 to 2 per cent of national output. With the diffusion of the Bessemer process, manufacturers were forced to increase scale. As a result, by 1880, the entire production of Bessemer steel came from just thirteen plants.[44] Between 1869 to 1899, capital invested in the US nearly tripled in constant dollars. Total annual factor productivity (TFR) growth[45], which had held steady at about 0.3% in the US throughout much of the 19th century, rose to 1.7% between 1889 and 1919. These unprecedented increase in industrial growth have been called the second industrial revolution.[46]

iii. One of the features of this period was **concentration** and **centralization of capital**, resulting in the rise of monopolies. A classic example of such a monopoly firm was **John D Rockefeller**'s **Standard Oil** trust, formed in 1882 out of a previously loose alliance of the major kerosene producers and refiners. The alliance already held a monopoly and controlled over 90% of American refineries and pipelines. It was a way of centralizing control through ownership so that economics of scale could be realized. Refineries were shut, others reorganized, and new ones opened so that all the oil could be forced to pass through a few large refineries. While the average refinery in 1880 had a daily capacity of 1500 to 2000 barrels of kerosene, Rockefeller plants had a capacity of 5,000 to 6,500 barrels of kerosene. And in 1886, the trust chose to build a plant in Lima, Ohio, that could process 36,000 barrels a day! So while the cost of production for plants of average size in 1885 was 1.5 cents per gallon, Standard Oil's cost was only 0.45 cent per gallon.[47]

iv. Working class movements in Europe gathered momentum and became a formidable force during this period. A part of colonial and monopoly super profits trickled down to workers of advanced capitalist countries, giving rise to the so-called labor aristocracy.

Piketty remembers **Eduard Bernstein** and his preparedness to become vice-president of the Reichstag, but forgets these vital developments and facts. In totality, this period marked a rise in global inequality.

Similarly, the period 1945-75 christened the **Trente Glorieuses**, was neither glorious nor peaceful. This period has in its background massive destruction of the Second World War (including the nuclear holocaust of Hiroshima and Nagasaki). And throughout this period, local wars from Korea to Congo, from Middle East to Vietnam, brutal suppression of national popular movements, CIA-sponsored regime changes, etc., continued unabated claiming millions of human lives.

TENDENCY OF RATE OF PROFIT TO FALL

Marx's theory regarding the 'tendency of general rate of profit to fall' is linked with his concept of the 'organic composition of capital'. "The composition of capital is to be understood in a two-fold sense. On the side of value, it is determined by the proportion in which it is divided into constant capital or value of the means of production, and variable capital or value of labor-power, the sum total of wages. On the side of material, as it functions in the process of production, all capital is divided into means of production and living labor-power. This latter composition is determined by the relation between the mass of the means of production employed, on the one hand, and the mass of labor necessary for their employment on the other.

I call the former the **value composition**, the latter the **technical composition** of capital. Between the two there is a strict correlation. To express this, I call the value composition of capital, in so far as it is determined by its technical composition and mirrors the changes of the latter, the **organic composition of capital**. Wherever I refer to the composition of capital, without further qualification, its organic composition is always understood."[48]

"The progressive tendency of the general rate of profit to fall is just **an expression peculiar to the capitalist mode of production** of the progressive development of the social productivity of labor. This does not mean to say that the rate of profit may not fall temporarily for other reasons. But proceeding from the nature of the capitalist mode of production, it is thereby proved a logical necessity that in its development the general average rate of surplus-value must express itself in a falling general rate of profit. Since the mass of the employed living labor is continually on the decline as compared to the mass of materialized labor set in motion by it, i.e., to the productively consumed means of production, it follows that the portion of living labor, unpaid and congealed in surplus-value, must also be continually on the decrease compared to the amount of value represented by the invested total capital. Since the ratio of the mass of surplus value to the value of the invested total capital forms the rate of profit, this rate must constantly fall. ...

The law that a fall in the rate of profit due to the development of productiveness is **accompanied by an increase in the mass of profit**, also expresses itself in the fact that a fall in the price of commodities produced by a capital is accompanied by a relative increase of the masses of profit contained in them and realized by their sale. ..

If we consider the enormous development of the productive forces of social labor in the last 30 years alone as compared with all preceding periods; if we consider, in particular, the enormous mass of fixed capital, aside from the actual machinery, which goes into the process of social production as a whole, then the difficulty which has hitherto troubled the economist, namely to explain the falling rate of profit, gives place to its opposite, namely to explain why this fall is not greater and more rapid. **There must be some counteracting influences at work, which cross and annul the effect of the general law, and which give it merely the CHARACTERISTIC OF A TENDENCY,** for which reason we have referred to the fall of the general rate of profit **as a tendency to fall**. ..

The following are the most general **counter-balancing forces**: i. Increasing intensity of exploitation; ii. Depression of wages below the value of labor-power; iii. Relative over-population; iv. Foreign trade (Is the general rate of profit raised by the higher rate of profit produced by capital invested in foreign and particularly colonial trade?); and v. Increase of the stock capital. .. The foregoing five points may still be supplemented by the following. .. With the progress of capitalist production, which goes hand in hand with accelerated accumulation, a portion of capital is calculated and applied only as **interest-bearing capital**. .. A fall in the rate of profit intensifies competitive struggle among capitalists, and hastens the **concentration and**

centralization of capital through expropriation of minor capitalists. ..."[49]

I think, no further explanation is required in this regard.

4. WEALTH INHERITED AND CREATED

"I was worshipping the god's temple, an ancient pile of stone. 'Lord of Thymbra, give us an enduring dwelling place; grant a house and family to thy weary servants and a city to abide: keep Troy's second fortress, the remnant left of the Grecians and merciless Achilles. Whom follow we? Or whither dost thou bid us go, where fix our seat? Grant an omen, O Lord, and inspire our minds.' Scarcely had I spoken thus, suddenly all seemed to shake, all the courts and laurels of the god, the whole hill to be stirred round about, and the caldron to moan in the opening sanctuary. We sink low in the ground, and a voice is borne to our ears: 'stubborn race of Dardanus, the same land that bore you by parentage of old shall receive you again on her bountiful breasts. **Seek out your ancient mother**; hence shall the house of **Aeneas** sway all regions, his children's children and they who shall be born of them. .. Then my father unrolling the records of men of old, 'Hear, O princes', says he, 'and learn your hopes. In mid ocean lies **Crete**, the island of high **Jove**, wherein is **Mount Ida**, the cradle of our race. .." Virgil, 'The Aeneid'.[50]

Millions of people all over the world today are dispossessed, displaced, and uprooted from their lands, water bodies, forests etc. due to industrialization, wars, partition, natural disasters, and are spending their lives in horrible conditions in temporary shelters and refugee camps. No divine voice reminds their children of their ancient mother and her bountiful breasts, of their Crete and Mount Ida. These dispossessions and displacements are creating future inheritances for a few. So, whenever we talk about large inheritances, we should remember the disinherited, dispossessed, displaced rootless millions.

In history, a large section of human population used to inherit debt of their ancestors (in other words, they have negative inheritance), and their slavery and serfdom. Slave and serf labor on the other hand created large inheritances of their lords. A slave child inherited from his/her parent slavery; **Thomas Jefferson** inherited more than 600 slaves from his father and father-in-law.

Workers without any inheritance have to eke out their living by selling labor-power. Some inherit so meager a property that is hardly sufficient for bare subsistence. Some others inherit earned income of their ancestors, and combined with their own living labor, are able to sustain a decent, or modest, or comparatively affluent living. The living labor of these workers and professionals (scientists, engineers, doctors, artists, etc.) keeps the economy going, provides the source of good return on inheritances.

And lastly, there are large, very, very large inheritances – most of them owe their origin to profiteering and robbery.

"The gypsy thought that there was no vulgar ambition then to possess bedrooms by the hundred. ... Looked at from the gypsy point of view, a Duke, Orlando understood, was nothing but a profiteer or robber who snatched land and money from people who rated these things of little worth, and could think of nothing better to do than build three hundred and sixty-five bedrooms when one was enough, and none was even better than one. She could not deny that her ancestors had accumulated field after field; house after house; honor after honor; yet had none of them been saints or heroes, or great benefactors of the human race. Nor could she counter the argument that any man who did now what her ancestors had done three or four hundred years ago would be denounced – and by her own family most loudly – for a vulgar upstart, an adventurer, a **nouveau riche**. .." Virginia Woolf, 'Orlando: A Biography'.[51]

This vulgar display of one's wealth is nothing new in this age of capital as well. Because of their size and past 'successes', large firms face limited competition. Instead of paying tremendous amounts of cash in their hands to their employees and investors, 'they waste it on pet projects, plush offices, executive jets or making an architectural statement with a new building .. a mausoleum to themselves. Examples of this kind of phenomenon are legion. **Phillipe Kahn** of Borland International (a front-ranking software maker) started building a $100 million headquarters – complete with a full size basketball court, pool, and two tennis courts – in 1992.'[52] Kahn's project was soon overshadowed by Indian billionaire **Mukesh Ambani**'s 'Antilia'.

Granted that supply and demand, differences in capital intensity and rates of profit in different countries, uneven economic development, diversified prudent investments etc., have important roles, but the primary source of return on inherited wealth/capital is the **living labor** of workers, of the dispossessed and the disinherited, of various sections of professionals. Only when seized and filled with a soul by living labor that inheritances increase with the advancing stages of accumulation. 'It is the natural property of living labor to transmit old value, whilst it creates new. Hence, with the increase in efficacy, extent and value of its means of production, consequently with the accumulation that accompanies the development of its productive power, labor keeps up and eternizes an always increasing capital-value in a form ever new. This natural power of labor takes the **appearance** of an intrinsic property of capital, in which it is incorporated. ..'[53]

Part Three of Piketty's book is dedicated to discussions on the relative importance of inherited wealth versus income from labor over the very long run. Providing valuable data and information on this subject, he takes the readers on to a ride into the interesting world of **Balzac** ('Père Goriot'), **Jane Austen** ('Sense and Sensibility'), **Henry James** ('Washington Square'), and **Orson Welles** ('The Magnificent Ambersons'). Inheritance too has been a subject of fierce debates since the advent of classical political economy. The demand to abolish the right of inheritance was put forward by **Saint-Simon**'s followers (**Enfantin, Bazard, Rodrigues, Buchez**, etc.) way back in late 1820s. In 1830, a book was published in Paris which, based as it was on Bazard's lectures, expressed the views of Saint-Simon's followers on the right of inheritance.[54] Later at the **Basle Congress** of the **First International** (6-11 September, 1869), the question of the right of inheritance was entered on the agenda at the suggestion of the Geneva Section headed by **Bakuninists**. They proposed to annihilate the right of inheritance believing this to be the only means of eliminating private property and social injustice.[55]

However, revolutions, wars, great depression, inflation wiped out much of the inherited wealth during the period

1914-50, particularly in Europe. Piketty writes, "During the decades that followed World War II, inherited wealth lost much of its importance, and for the first time in history, perhaps, work and study became the surest routes to the top. Today, even though all sorts of inequalities have re-emerged, and many beliefs in social and democratic progress have been shaken, most people still believe that the world has changed radically since **Vautrine** lectured **Rastignac**. .. In the vast majority of cases, however, **it is not only more moral but also more profitable to rely on study, work, and professional success**." (Chapter Seven/ Inequality and Concentration: Preliminary Bearings)

Moreover, he warns, "**If, for example, the top docile appropriates 90% of each year's output (and the top centile took 50% just for itself, as in the case of wealth), a revolution will likely occur, unless some peculiarly effective repressive apparatus exists to keep it from happening. When it comes to the ownership of capital, such a high degree of concentration is already a source of powerful political tensions, which are often difficult to reconcile with universal suffrage**. .. Indeed, whether such extreme inequality is or is not sustainable depends not only on the effectiveness of the repressive apparatus but also, and perhaps primarily, on the effectiveness of the apparatus of justification. **If inequalities are seen as justified, say because they seem to be a consequence of a choice by the rich to work harder or more efficiently than the poor, or because preventing the rich from earning more would inevitably harm the worst-off members of society, then it is perfectly possible for the concentration of income to set new historical records.**

That is why I indicate in Table 7.3 that the US may set a new record around 2030 if inequality of income from labor – and to a lesser extent inequality of ownership of capital – continues to increase as they have done in recent decades. The top docile would then claim about 60% of national income, while the bottom half would get barely 15%. .. I want to insist on this point: **the key issue is the justification of inequalities rather than their magnitude as such**. ..

SUPER-MANAGERS AND SUPER-SALARIES

Piketty further writes, "The first of .. two ways of achieving such high inequality is through a '**hyper-patrimonial society**' (or a '**society of rentiers**'): a society in which inherited wealth is very important and where the concentration of wealth attains extreme levels (with the upper docile owning typically 90% of all wealth, with 50% belonging to the upper centile alone). The total income hierarchy is then dominated by very incomes from capital, especially inherited capital. ..

The second way of achieving such high inequality is relatively new. It was largely created by the US over the past few decades. Here we see that a very high level of total income inequality can be the result of '**hyper-meritocratic society**' (or at any rate a society that the people at the top like to describe as hyper-meritocratic). One might also call this a '**society of superstars**' (or perhaps '**super-managers**', a somewhat different characterization). In other words, this is a very inegalitarian society, but **one in which the peak of the income hierarchy is dominated by very high incomes from labor rather than by inherited**

wealth. ... At this point, it will suffice to note that the stark contrast I have drawn here between two types of hyper-inegalitarian society – a society of rentiers and a society of super-managers – is naïve and overdrawn. The two types of inequality can co-exist: there is no reason why a person cannot be both a super-manager and a rentier – and the fact that the concentration of wealth is currently much higher in the US than in Europe suggests that this may well be the case in the US today. And, of course, there is **nothing to prevent the children of super-managers from being rentiers**. In practice, we find both logics at work in every society. .." (Chapter Seven/Inequality of Total Income: Two Worlds)

Super-salaries of these super-managers defy any explanation on the basis of the **theory of marginal productivity**. Piketty admits, '**The very notion of 'individual marginal productivity' becomes hard to define. In fact, it becomes SOMETHING CLOSER TO A PURE IDEOLOGICAL CONSTRUCT ON THE BASIS OF WHICH A JUSTIFICATION FOR HIGHER STATUS CAN BE ELABORATED**."

Warning against such justification, he further writes, "In the United States in recent years, one frequently has heard this type of justification (defense of meritocracy) for the stratospheric pay of super-managers (50-100 times average income; if not more). Proponents of such high pay argued that without it, only the heirs of large fortunes would be able to achieve true wealth, which would be unfair. In the end, therefore, the millions or tens of millions of dollars a year paid to super-managers contribute to greater social justice. This kind of argument could well lay the groundwork for greater and more violent inequality in the future. The world to come may well combine the worst of two past worlds: both very large inequality of inherited wealth and very high wage inequalities justified in terms of merit and productivity (claims with very little factual basis, as noted). **Meritocratic extremism can thus lead to a race between super-managers and rentiers, to the detriment of those who are neither.**" (Chapter Eleven/Merit and Inheritance in the Long Run/Meritocratic Extremism in Wealthy Societies).

Thus, the theory of marginal productivity fails Piketty, but the way out of this 'pure ideological construct', lies, as we have seen before, in explaining the super-salaries of these super-managers as '**profit of the firm or enterprise**', and hence, as part of **capital income** (instead of labor income). With the financialization and socialization of capital, there appears the **duality of capital proper and functioning capital, and of interest and profit of the enterprise/firm.** This duality creates illusion of which Piketty is a victim. The capitalist entrepreneur, as distinct from the owner of capital, does not appear as operating capital, but rather as a functionary irrespective of capital, or as a simple agent of the labor-process in general, as a laborer, and indeed as a salaried laborer. Similarly, interest on capital lends other portion of profit (profit of enterprise) as wages of superintendence. I have already dealt with this subject in the earlier part of the critique.

Piketty persists with this illusion and hence, despite his reservations, fails to effectively challenge the justification for these super-salaries in terms of merit and productivity.

However, with the advent of new technologies, new organizational forms become necessary. Until around the middle of 19th century, most firms were managed by their owners – **Eric Hobsbawm** contrasted the 150 top families in Bordeaux (France) in 1848 with the top 450 families in the same region in 1960 and found that the largest group in the latter period, the salaried business executives was completely absent.[56]

In the latter half of the 19th century, 'as **Alfred Chandler** argues, advances in transportation (in particular, the advent of the railways) and in communication (the telegraph) made possible larger markets for goods. The large volume of goods that were required allowed manufacturers to amortize set up costs and capital investment quickly. As a result, large, capital-intensive manufacturing units sprang up to exploit technologies that could realize lower per unit costs than smaller outfits. In this background, new organizational form emerged: large, vertically integrated firms that Chandler calls the modern business enterprise. And with this new organizational form emerged a class of salaried business managers.'[57]

In 1941, American philosopher **J Burnham** (1905-1987) propounded the theory of '**Managerial Revolution**', which seems to be behind placing super-managers in the category of laborers. Burnham maintained that with the development of capitalist production, the class of capitalists becomes increasingly isolated from direct economic activities and management of enterprises. The functions of organizing and managing the economic, and then, the whole life of society are gradually assumed by a new social stratum, the managers, a sector of the broad working class. Therefore, the gradual ousting of capitalist owners and the increasing role of the technocrats, or managers, will result in a change in the nature of the entire social order.

For the term 'meritocratic' (which is advanced in defense of super-salaries), we can well go back to American sociologist **Daniel Bell**'s theory of **post-industrial society**. Bell's post-industrial society is supposed to be founded not on the production of material benefits, but on the scientific institutions, on a kind of scientific and administrative complex wielding great influence, and hence, the key decision-making process is being gradually assumed by talented scientists promoted by all sections of society – which he terms as **meritocracy**.

In the latter half of the 20th century, due to computer revolution, necessity of new organizational forms provided the basis for the emergence of super-salaried super-managers. Computer revolution led to the restructuring of industrial production, and most prominently, to the emergence of a variety of financial instruments.

"Entire new markets such as NASDAQ have emerged catering specifically to young firms. Institutions such as money market funds did not exist in early 1970s. A large number of financial derivatives that are commonplace today, such as index options or interest rate swaps, have not yet been invented three decades ago. The turnover in the trading of such derivative instruments was $163 trillion in the fourth quarter of 2001, about 16 times the annual GDP of the United States. .. Revolving consumer credit such as credit card debt has exploded from near nothing in the US

in the late 1960s to nearly $700 billion in late 2001. ..
Gross cross-border capital flows as a fraction of GDP have
increased nearly tenfold in developed countries since 1970
and more than fivefold for developing countries. In the
decade of 1990s alone, these flows more than quadrupled
for developed countries. .. In 1979, the US Department of
Labor finally clarified the concept of prudence: risky
investments were deemed legitimate if they were part of a
well-diversified portfolio strategy. As a result of this
decision, pension funds and large endowments were able to
start investing in riskier intermediaries such as **venture
capital funds** (which finance start-up companies), **buyout
funds** (which finance the acquisition of existing
companies), and '**vulture funds**' (which buy debt of
financially distressed firms while hoping to profit from
their restructuring). This new market, called the private
equity market, emerged and grew with breathtaking speed.
While in 1980 the US private equity market accounted for
only $5 billion in investment, in 1999 it was over $175
billion. This roughly equal to the total amount of
investment made annually by a country like Italy, the fifth
biggest economy in the world. .. In 2000, venture capitalists
channeled more than $100 billion into 5,608 new
companies. In 2001, even after the collapse of euphoria
about the Internet, 3,244 companies obtained more than
$38 billion in venture capital finance. Only ten years
earlier, the total amount financed was just $3 billion spread
over 1,143 companies. .. From 1980 to 2000, the fraction of
public equity owned by institutional investors in the US
went from below 30% to over 60%, while the fraction
owned by individuals declined in tandem. The number of

mutual funds increased from 564 in 1980 to 8,171 in 2000. There are now more mutual funds in existence in the US than there are domestic companies listed on US stock exchanges! .. Substantial increase took place in the average rate of return on corporate assets. While in 1980, it had dropped as low as 5.7%, by 1996, it was a healthy 9.9%. ..",58 ..

I think this is enough to understand the background behind the phenomenon of super-salaries and super-managers in the US. Needless to say that there is a vast difference between these super-managers (CEOs, COOs, CFOs, CTOs, directors, etc.) and lower level managers (doing almost clerical jobs). While the former claims profit of the firm/enterprise, the latter sections have to do with their wages only.

Apart from industrial and financial firms, this phenomenon of superstars-super-managers-super-salaries can be observed in professional firms (like medical, engineering, educational, law, consultancy, music/entertainment, and similar firms) as well as in many non-governmental organizations (NGOs) engaged in social sector. Superstar doctors, engineers, educationists/academicians, lawyers, actors and performers, musicians, social activists/entrepreneurs, top executives of NGOs etc. (some of them may be owners or partners of their respective firms), claim **profit** of their firms, while their employees – doctors, engineers, teachers, lawyers, actors, musicians etc., have to remain content with their **wages**.

ENTREPRENEUR AND RENTIER

Accumulated wealth tends to follow the formula $M \to M'$. When **Tom Sawyer** and **Huck** found the money that the robbers hid in the cave, it made them rich – they got six thousand dollars apiece, all gold. It was an awful sight of money when it was piled up. What did they do with that money? They took it to Judge **Thatcher** who put it out at interest, and it fetched Tom and Huck a dollar a day apiece, all the year round – 'more than a body could tell what to do with.'[59]

In the ancient and medieval world, it took the form of usury; in the age of capital, it takes the form of financialization. 'There is no reason why a person cannot be both a super-manager and a rentier. .. There is nothing to prevent the children of entrepreneur or super-managers from becoming rentiers.' In the earlier part of this critique, this tendency of capital is discussed in detail. Since in bourgeois economics entrepreneurial income (or super-salaries of super-managers) is designated as **income from labor**, it is extolled as virtuous, morally correct. Rentiers' income is derided as morally degrading leading towards a highly inegalitarian patrimonial society, instead of building a meritocratic society based on justifiable inequalities. As we have observed, Piketty here offers nothing new (George Ramsay expressed similar fears in case of England almost one hundred seventy-eight years ago, and he too included entrepreneurial activity in the category of labor).

Bernick: .. Fifteen years ago, I was the guilty man. ..

(To his son Olaf): In future you shall be allowed to grow up, not as the inheritor of my life-work, but as someone who has a life-work of his own to look forward to.

Olaf: And will you let me be whatever I want to?

Bernick: Yes, you shall.

Olaf: Thank you. Then I won't be a pillar of the community.

Bernick: No? Why not?

Olaf: Because I think that must be so dull. ..

Bernick: .. I have learnt that, too, these last days; it is women who are the pillars of the community.

Miss Hessel: Then you have learnt a poor kind of wisdom, my dear man. [Laying her hands firmly on his shoulders] No, my dear: the spirit of truth and the spirit of freedom, they are the pillars of the community.

Henrik Ibsen, 'The Pillars of the Community'.[60]

Piketty is well aware that within the capitalist mode of production, this tendency of capital (entrepreneurs turning into rentiers) cannot be checked. He writes, "The inequality $r > g$, combined with the inequality of returns on capital as function of initial wealth, can lead to excessive and lasting concentration of capital: no matter how justified inequalities of wealth may be initially, fortunes can now grow and perpetuate themselves beyond all reasonable limits and beyond any possible rational justification in terms of social utility. Entrepreneurs thus tend to turn into rentiers, not only with the passing of generations, but even within a single lifetime." (Chapter Twelve/ The Moral Hierarchy of Wealth)

Further, "One conclusion is already quite clear; however: **it is an illusion to think that something about the nature of modern growth or the laws of the market economy ensures that inequality of wealth will decrease and harmonious stability will be achieved.** (Chapter Ten/ Inequality of Capital Ownership/Hyperconcentrated Wealth: Europe and America) .. "The idea that unrestricted competition will put an end to inheritance and move toward a more meritocratic world is a **dangerous illusion**. The advent of universal suffrage and the end of property qualifications for voting ended the legal domination of politics by the wealthy. **But it did not abolish the economic forces capable of producing a society of rentiers.**" (Chapter Eleven/Merit and Inheritance in the Long Run/The Rentier, Enemy of Democracy)

On the moral hierarchy of wealth, Piketty is again confronted with the limits of the theory of marginal productivity. See this interesting passage from the book: "It is rather common to contrast the man who is currently the world's wealthiest, **Carlos Slim**, a Mexican real estate and telecom tycoon who is of Lebanese extraction and is often described in the Western press as one who owes his great wealth to monopoly rents obtained through (implicit corrupt) government favors, and **Bill Gates**, the former number one, who is seen as a model of the meritorious entrepreneur. At times one almost has the impression that Bill Gates himself invented computer science and the microprocessor and that he would be 10 times richer still if he had been paid his full **marginal productivity** and compensated for his personal contribution to global well-being. .. No doubt **the veritable cult of Bill Gates is an**

outgrowth of the apparently irrepressible need of modern democratic societies to make sense of inequality. To be frank, I know virtually nothing about exactly how Carlos Slim or Bill Gates became rich, and I am quite incapable of assessing their relative merits. Nevertheless, it seems to me that Bill Gates also profited from a virtual monopoly on operating systems (as have many other high-tech entrepreneurs in industries ranging from telecommunications to **Facebook**, whose fortunes were also built on monopoly rents). Furthermore, I believe that Gates's contributions depended on the work of thousands of engineers and scientists doing basic research in electronics and computer science, without whom none of his innovations would have been possible. These people did not patent their scientific papers. In short, it seems unreasonable to draw such an extreme contrast between Gates and Slim without so much as a glance at the facts. .. Rather than indulge in constructing a moral hierarchy of wealth, which in practice often amounts to an exercise in Western ethnocentrism, I think it is more useful to try to understand the general laws that govern the dynamics of wealth. .. At the very least, the reader will grant that these various cases are not fundamentally different but belong to a continuum, and that a fortune is often deemed more suspect if its owner is black. .." (Chapter Twelve/Global Inequality of Wealth in the Twenty-First Century/The Moral Hierarchy of Wealth) Well said indeed.

However, despite being aware of the limitations of the theory of marginal productivity, he refuses to allow living labor (and its unpaid labor-time) any role in the return on capital. He sticks to his basic premise (as mentioned in the earlier part of this critique). He writes, "Broadly speaking, the central fact is that the return on capital often inextricably combines elements of true entrepreneurial labor (an absolutely indispensable force for economic development), pure luck (one happens at the right moment to buy a promising asset at a good price), and outright theft. .." (Ibid)

TRANSCENDING CAPITAL

Piketty is well aware that 'there is no guarantee that distribution of inherited capital will not ultimately become as inegalitarian in the 21st century as it was in the 19th. .. There is no ineluctable force standing in the way of a return to extreme concentration of wealth. .. If the top docile appropriates 90% of each year's output (and the top centile took 50% just for itself, as in the case of wealth), a revolution will likely occur, unless some peculiarly effective repressive apparatus exists to keep it from happening. .. The crisis of 2008 was the first crisis of the globalized patrimonial capitalism of the twenty-first century. It is unlikely to be the last.' Since this problem of concentration of wealth and the resultant crisis cannot be resolved within the confines of capitalist mode of production, he even 'imagines' of '**transcending capitalism**' – 'Can we imagine a 21st century in which capitalism will be transcended in a more peaceful and more lasting way, or must we simply await the next crisis or the next war (this time truly global)?' (Chapter Thirteen/A Social State for the Twenty-First Century)

He further writes, "**The solution to the problem of capital suggested by Karl Marx and many other socialist**

writers in the 19th century and put into practice in the Soviet Union and elsewhere in the 20th century was far more radical and, if nothing else, **more logically consistent**. .. By abolishing private ownership of the means of production, Soviet experiment simultaneously eliminated all private returns on capital. The rate of exploitation, which for Marx represented the share of output appropriated by the capitalist thus fell to zero, and with it the rate of private return. With zero return on capital, man (or worker) finally threw off his chains along with the yoke of accumulated wealth. **The present reasserted its rights over the past**. The inequality r > g was nothing but a bad memory, especially since communism vaunted its affection for growth and technological progress. .. The problem was that private property and the market economy do not serve solely to ensure the domination of capital over those who have nothing to sell but their labor-power. They also play a useful role in coordinating the actions of millions of individuals, and it is not so easy to do without them. .." (Chapter Fifteen/A Global Tax on Capital)

Here, we cannot go into the examination of Soviet experiment regarding 'transcending capitalism'. The point is, even after finding Marx's and other socialists' suggestion logically consistent, Piketty, presenting the failure of Soviet experiment as an instance, refuses to venture into the challenging field of 'transcending capitalism'. Instead of putting forward any new insight and suggesting any new experiment based on previous experiences, he simply closes this option.

The other option of **making capitalism stable, balanced and harmonious is already closed**. He time and again makes it clear that he does not believe in such illusions. Experiments to make capitalism stable, balanced and harmonious during the last three centuries have been proved to be more disastrous and devastating. He does not want to attempt any new experiment in this regard as well.

So, what should be done? A stable, balanced and harmonious capitalism is impossible, and transcending capitalism too is not feasible. Piketty suggests, let capitalism function the way it functions, only regulate and control it so that it does not meet a violent end. He suggests a **controlled capitalism – taming of capital going wild**. He is reconciled to a future of 'patrimonial capitalism', like the patrimonial feudalism of the past, and just wants to prevent it from developing into a 'hyper-patrimonial society'.

PROGRESSIVE GLOBAL TAX ON CAPITAL

He writes, "**A tax on capital would be a less violent and more efficient response to the eternal problem of private capital and its return**. A progressive levy on individual wealth would **re-assert control over capitalism** in the name of general interest while relying on the forces of private property and competition." (Chapter Fifteen) .. "But if democracy is to regain control over the globalized financial capitalism of this century, it must also invent new tools, adapted to today's challenges. The ideal tool would be a progressive global tax on capital, coupled with a very high level of international financial transparency. Such a tax would provide a way to avoid an endless inegalitarian spiral and to control the worrisome dynamics of global capital concentration." (Ibid) .. "The progressive tax is a crucial component of the social state. .. The progressive tax is thus a relatively liberal method for reducing inequality, in the sense that free competition and private property are respected while private incentives are modified in potentially radical ways, but always according to rules thrashed out in democratic debate. The progressive tax thus represents an ideal compromise between social justice and individual freedom. .." (Chapter Fourteen/Rethinking the Progressive Income Tax) .. "A progressive tax on capital is a more suitable instrument for responding to the challenges of the 21st century than a progressive income tax." (Chapter Thirteen/A Social State for the Twenty-First Century)

Piketty is also aware of the limitations of his proposal. For him, a stable, balanced and harmonious capitalism is a **utopia**, transcending capitalism too is a **utopia**, but his own proposal of a global tax on capital is a **useful utopia worth trying**.

In the face of three centuries of objective data that unequivocally provide useful objective lessons regarding the movement of capital accumulation, Piketty instead of pursuing those lessons further, settles for a **useful utopia**. **Data, in Piketty's hands, degrades into a delusional utopia**.

Capitalism is a mode of production based on exchange. Division of labor, exchange, trade and usury have been in existence since ancient times, but **exchange-based mode of production** (as we have already seen) became a reality only after the advent of industrial capital, and soon it replaced the **land-based feudal mode of production** as the dominant mode all over the world. Exchange is based on the law of value, hence transcending capitalism means **transcending exchange and law of value**. It is during exchange that surplus-value is created and that is the source of capital accumulation. Since exchange-based economy remains in operation even during wars, crisis and calamities, hence despite setbacks, periodic fluctuations, capitalism continues to flourish. Different sectors or departments of capital assume prominence during different conditions (e.g., military-industrial complex during wars). It just cannot be wished away – pious condemnation or subjective efforts or administrative steps cannot check capital accumulation. Even in extreme cases of capital controls, it temporarily may go underground only to reappear with vengeance at a later date. However, in course of its development, it itself creates and expands objective conditions and factors for its own transcendence. Here it is not possible to go into its details.

Capital is a flow, and in its continuous movement around the world in different terrains and environments, it takes in its embrace everything that comes in its way – private small savings, large inheritances, pension funds, tax revenues, sovereign wealth funds, etc., invests them in different financial instruments and seeks to get better and better returns.

Government's subsidies and social spending on education, health, insurance, etc., becomes part of this capital circulation. A lot of educational, medical, insurance, construction, etc., firms actually flourish on government's social sector spending. All corporate houses now have diversified in different fields and grab a large part of government's social spending. All money temporarily **withdrawn** (or taken away) from this circulation through taxes, etc., finally **return** to it – that may result in a somewhat redistribution of capital among its different constituents.

So, a progressive tax on capital is destined to return to capital in different forms. Moreover, capitalists have, over the past three centuries, mastered the art of tax evasion – Piketty himself suggests a revision of his capital/income ratio in view (although it is a very modest view) of this tax evasion – 'It turns out that we need to add several percentage points to capital income's share of national income (perhaps as many as 5 percentage points if we choose a high estimate of tax evasion, but more realistically 2 to 3 percent points). This is not a negligible amount.' (Chapter Eight/Two Worlds)

WEALTH INHERITED AND CREATED

Inheritance, wars over inheritances, dispossession, search for new lands, creation of new kingdoms have been subjects of great epics, both eastern and western. Throughout history, inherited wealth has often changed hands due to the rise of new economic forces, due to rebellions and revolutions, due to wars, and other factors. With the rise of agrarian communities, tribes were restructured on the basis of feudal mode of production and tribal wealth was transformed into feudal property. Throughout the agrarian period spread over thousands of years, due to rise of new kingdoms and empires, and frequent wars, feudal inheritances regularly changed hands.

The advent of capital led to the restructuring of agrarian societies and feudal property was transformed into capitalist property. The promulgation of the 1534 Act of Supremacy, which proclaimed the king head of the Church, was followed in England by the confiscation of Catholic Church lands and property in favor of the king and dissolution of the monasteries, sanctioned by the Parliamentary acts of 1536 and 1539. In France, after the revolution of 1848, 'freed from court and representation costs at Paris, landholders had, out of the very corners of provinces, only to gather the golden apples falling into their châteaux from the tree of modern industry, railways enhancing the price of their land, agronomy applied to it by capitalist farmers, increasing its produce, and the inexhaustible demand of a rapidly swollen town population, securing the growth of markets for that produce.'[61] Under the colonial system, large inheritances of tribal communities and feudal kingdoms in colonial countries were (through loot, plunder, unequal trade, etc.) converted into capitalist property of the colonizing countries – guess how much west African and Indian inheritances got metamorphosed into French and British capital? This process is still going on in different ways and with different actors.

Remember if, on one end of the spectrum, inherited wealth forms the large, very large component of accumulated capital in Europe and the United States, then, on the other end, there are very large countries like China where inherited wealth has yet to make its mark. In China, Russia, East European countries, etc., world's largest number of first generation capitalist millionaires and billionaires are emerging – these are countries where revolution has wiped out all inheritances of the earlier period and private property and capitalist enterprises emerged only in eighties and nineties. Hence, in what way does the composition of global inherited wealth get reconstituted in the 21st century is anybody's guess.

Moreover, the computer revolution has itself created and is still creating a new generation of billionaires in the US and other developed and developing countries (India, Ireland, Brazil, Mexico, Indonesia, South Africa, Turkey, Vietnam, Philippines, etc.), and much of the inherited wealth in these countries is passing into the hands of these new first generation billionaires. Capitalism has since long converted wealth (material and cultural) generated thousands of years ago during Mesolithic and Neolithic period (not to say of the wealth created during the Middle Ages) into capitalist property – Pyramids, Stonehenge, or Lascaux cave paintings are now part of the billions of dollars of tourist industry as well as of a number of other trades. Ancient artifacts are now part of the antique business (legal as well as illegal). Codex Leicester (named after its eighteenth-century owner Thomas Coke, Earl of Leicester), the most unified of **Leonardo da Vinci**'s notebooks is now owned by Bill Gates.[62]

5. CENTURY TWENTIETH AND TWENTY-FIRST

"Your Malebranche," said Huron to Gordon one day, "seems to have written half of his book whilst he was in possession of his reason, and the other half with the assistance only of imagination and prejudice."

Voltaire, 'Master Simple'.[63]

Twentieth century was the century of some epoch-making developments, heralding a new chapter in the history of humankind. These developments provide the key to understand the shape of things to come in the twenty-first century. A quick look into these developments, hence, will not be out of place.

A. Mechanization and its consequences: The 'second industrial revolution' in the latter half of the nineteenth century led to the development of large-scale industries, to a spurt in ever-increasing mechanization, to monopoly finance capital and emergence of transnational corporations, to a new wave of colonization, and to a new class of business executives and labor aristocracy during the period, 1870-1913. These developments became the characteristic features of twentieth century capitalism. Moreover, it was in this century that the **military-industrial complex** in advanced capitalist countries acquired a major role in both diplomacy and domestic politics.

We can, here, briefly go into the consequences of mechanization in order to grasp the development in the latter half of the twentieth century.

"To the degree that large industry develops, the creation of real wealth comes to depend less on labor time and on the amount of labor employed then on the power of the agencies set in motion during labor time, whose 'powerful effectiveness' is itself in turn out of all proportions to the direct labor time spent on their production, but rather on the general state of science and on the progress of technology, or the application of this science to production (especially natural sciences, and all others with the latter, is itself in turn related to the development of material production.) .. **Labor no longer appears so much to be included within the production process; rather, the human being comes to relate more as watchman and regulator to the production process itself.** .. He steps to the side of the production process instead of being its chief actor. In this transformation, it is neither the direct human labor he himself performs, nor the time during which he works, but rather the appropriation of his own general productive power, his understanding of nature and his mastery over it by virtue of his presence as a social body – it is, in a word, the development of the social individual which appears as the great foundation-stone of production and of wealth. **The theft of alien labor time, on which the present wealth is based**, appears a miserable foundation in face of this new one, created by large-scale industry itself. As soon as labor in the direct form has ceased to be the great well-spring of wealth, labor time ceases and must cease to be its measure, and hence exchange value (must cease to be the measure) of use value. **The surplus labor of the mass has ceased to be the condition for the development of general wealth, just as the non-labor of the few, for the development of the general powers of the human head. With that, production based on exchange value breaks down, and the direct, material production process is stripped of the form of penury and anti-thesis.** The free development of individualities, and hence the reduction of necessary labor time so as to posit surplus labor, but rather the general reduction of the necessary labor of society to a minimum, which then corresponds to the artistic, scientific etc. development of the individuals in the **time set free**, and with the means created, for all of them. **Capital itself is the moving contradiction, (in) that it presses to reduce labor time to a minimum, while it posits labor time, on the other side, as sole measure and source of wealth. Hence it diminishes labor time in the necessary form so as to increase it in the superfluous form; hence posits the superfluous in growing measure as a condition – question of life or death – for the necessary.** On the one side, then, it calls to life all the powers of science and of nature, as of social combination and of social intercourse, in order to make the creation of wealth independent (relatively) of the labor time employed on it. On the other side, it wants to use labor time as the measuring rod for the giant social forces thereby created, and to confine them within the limits required to maintain the already created value as value. Forces of production and social relations –

two different sides of the development of the social individual – appear to capital as mere means, and are merely means for it to produce on its limited foundation. In fact, however, they are **the material conditions to blow this foundation sky-high**. 'Truly wealthy a nation, when the working day is 6 rather than 12 hours. **Wealth is not command over surplus labor time (real wealth), but rather, disposable time outside that needed in direct production, for every individual and the whole society.**'

Nature builds no machines, no locomotives, railways, electric telegraphs, self-acting mules etc. These are products of human industry; natural material transformed into organs of the human will over nature, or of human participation in nature. They are **organs of the human brain, created by the human hand; the power of knowledge objectified. The development of fixed capital indicates to what degree general social knowledge has become a direct force of production, and to what degree, hence, the conditions of the process of social life itself have come under the control of the general intellect and been transformed in accordance with it.** To what degree the powers of social production have been produced, not only in the form of knowledge, but also as immediate organs of social practice, of the real life process. ..

The saving of labor time (is) equal to an increase of free time, i.e. time for the full development of the individual, which in turn reacts back upon the productive power of labor as itself the greatest productive power. .. Free time – which is both idle time and time for higher

activity – has naturally transformed its possessor into a different subject, and he then enters into the direct production process as this different subject. ..”[64]

Remember, Marx wrote these lines 156 years ago. Piketty should note this passage since he writes in Chapter Six (The Capital-Labor Split in the Twenty-First Century/Back to Marx and the Falling Rate of Profit), "Today we know that long-term structural growth is possible only because of productivity growth. But this was not obvious in Marx's time, owing to lack of historical perspective and good data. .. In Marx's mind .. the very idea of structural growth driven by permanent and durable growth of productivity, was not clearly identified or formulated."

B. Revolution in science and technology: In the first decade of the twentieth century, two German scientists revolutionized our understanding of atomic-subatomic process as well as that of space-time, and thus laid the foundation of a new scientific and technological revolution that went on to radically change the way we think, read and write, research, produce and design, trade and shop, manage, communicate and campaign, save, invest and finance, spy, make war and peace, love and hate, befriend and unfriend, play and entertain, etc. in the coming decades.

One was **Max Karl Ernst Ludwig Planck**, born (at Kiel) in the Duchy of Holstein on April 23, 1858, who presented his **Quantum Theory** on December 14, 1900; and the other was, of course, **Albert Einstein**, born (at Ulm) in the Kingdom of Württemberg on March 14, 1879, who propounded his **special theory of relativity** in 1905 (and in

1916 formulated the **general theory of relativity**). This scientific revolution soon embraced other branches of science and led to the development of new instruments and gadgets. A continuous process of discovery-invention-innovation was ushered in. The Newtonian mechanical-deterministic world-view was replaced by a new world-view of relativity, probability and uncertainty, and this view influenced all the disciplines of humanities as well. Remember, this epoch-making revolution in science was taking place at the time when capitalism was undergoing a period of severe shocks (Piketty, as mentioned earlier, describes this period, 1913-1950, as 'the history of Europe's suicide, and in particular of the euthanasia of European capitalists').

C. Computer revolution and knowledge economy: This revolution in science led to the computer revolution of the second half of the twentieth century, and this computer revolution necessitated restructuring of production, organization and management of industrial capital, as well as it gave birth to a host of new financial instruments. **Knowledge as a factor of production rose in prominence.** Side by side, a new discipline of **knowledge economy** grew in importance.

"The knowledge economy stands on three pillars. The first: knowledge has become what we buy, sell, and do. It is the most important factor of production. The second pillar is a mate, a corollary to the first: knowledge assets – that is, intellectual capital – have become more important to companies than financial and physical assets. The third pillar is this: to prosper in this new economy and exploit these newly vital assets, we need new vocabularies, new management techniques, new technologies, and new strategies. On these pillars rest all the new economy's laws and its profits. .. When the idea of a 'new economy' was controversial, economists puzzled over the seeming failure of investment in information technology to produce gains in productivity. These doubts are – or should be – laid to rest now. Since 1994, US productivity (probably underestimated) has grown at a 2.8 per cent annual clip, double the average growth rate of the previous two decades. More than half that increase is attributable to information technology, including software – though IT capital stock is just one per cent of all capital stock. Ubiquitous ever-cheaper, ever more powerful information technology has unleashed a torrent of economic good. Why so powerful? First information is a factor of production in every industry, from farming to pharmaceuticals. Improve the efficiency with which information is used, and the innovation can be applied everywhere. .. Network externalities also turbo-charge the effects of gains in the use of knowledge. In addition, the skills demanded of knowledge workers require investments in human capital – so the workforce is becoming more skilled, and is able to apply its skills in unplanned-for ways. .. Finally, .. to take advantage of information technology and to become a true knowledge company requires new organizational forms – that is, to get the most out of new technology and intangible assets, companies often have to re-think their business model and their organizational design, producing 'a round of organizational innovation.' **Thus technical innovation feeds into social innovation, which feeds into more**

technical innovation, increasing the value of knowledge assets in a virtuous spiral. .. Ultimately, intellectual assets have become more important than any other because only by means of knowledge can companies differentiate their work from their competitors. Other sources of competitive advantage are rapidly drying up: geography (weakened by electronic commerce and reduced tariffs and lower barriers to foreign direct investment), regulation (which once insulated enormous sectors – transportation, communications, power, and financial services), and vertical integration (less valuable because more and more companies are finding it cheaper to buy on the open market what they once made themselves). You don't need physical assets to gain entry into a business. The specific asset – the differentiating asset – is not the machinery. **It's the software and the wetware – the stuff between your ears. It's the knowledge, stupid.** .. In the spring of 2001, Deutsche Bank took out a big ad in the **Wall Street Journal**. Its headline: '**Ideas are Capital. The Rest is Just Money.**'[65]

D. New time: Mechanization, revolution in science, and computer revolution have led to the development of a new age in the latter half of the 20th century, particularly since the last decade of that century during which the consumption of the goods and services produced by computer revolution became a mass phenomenon. This development has been described by various thinkers and writers in different ways. Some call it 'Capital 3.0'[66], some others describe it as 'knowledge society', or as 'digital age'.

That it is a new age can be well understood by its two defining characteristics. First, this new economy (while led to the restructuring of industry and finance) seeks to **command and control the socially available free time** through its gadgets, applications and services. (The industrial capital seeks to command and control socially available labor time, and finance capital seeks to command and control socially available savings.) Second, this new economy is changing the way we live: one of the surest ways to assess this change is to observe **how we spend our time**. In this age, billions of people worldwide spend a significant portion of their time on computers. "Television, computers, and smart phones compose a trifecta offering nearly constant interaction with a screen throughout the day. Human interactions in the physical world are now pushed relentlessly into the virtual world of networked devices. Recent studies suggest the adult Americans spend on average roughly half of their waking hours in front of a screen, and the figure continues to grow."[67] How this state of affairs is impacting the entire gamut of our lives is the subject-matter of a range of sociological and cultural studies. It would have been very beneficial to go into the impact of this new economy on state structure, governance, political processes as a whole, sovereignty, and on popular movements in a broader historical perspective; however, it is beyond the scope of this critique. Here, we can just have a glimpse of the world of Google.

"Google's colorful, playful logo is imprinted on human retinas just under 6 billion times each day, 2.1 trillion times a year – an opportunity for respondent conditioning enjoyed by no other company in history. .. The success of

Google's mobile operating system Android, launched in 2008, has given Google an 80% share of the smart phone market. Google claims that over a billion Android devices have registered themselves, at a rate now of more than a million new devices a day. Through Android, Google controls devices people carry on their daily routine and use to connect to the internet. Each device feeds back usage statistics, location, and other data to Google. This gives the company unprecedented power to surveil and influence the activities of its user base, both over network and as they go about their lives. Other Google projects such as 'Project Glass' and 'Project Tango' aim to build on Android's ubiquity, extending Google's surveillance capabilities farther into space around their users. Google is also aiming to become an internet access provider. Google's 'Project Loon' aims to provide internet access to populations in the global south using wireless access points mounted on fleets of high-altitude balloons and aerial drones, having acquired the drone companies Titan Aerospace and Makani Power. Facebook, which bid against Google for Titan Aerospace, has similar aspirations, having acquired the UK-based aerial drone company Ascenta."[68]

This new economy is creating more wealth at a speed unheard-of in history, giving birth to new billionaires and new inequalities. Yet it is the least taxed sector. As Thomas A Steward writes, "Knowledge assets fly under the tax man's radar just as they do the manager's. ... We can look at taxation as an indication of how little attention we pay to the real sources of wealth. Take property taxes, for decades a primary tool for generating tax revenue from business. Microsoft owns a big campus, but the value of its real estate is nothing compared to the value of its un-real estate. King County, Washington, assesses Microsoft's property at $1.05 billion, about 0.2 per cent of the market value of the company, as a whole, which is about $500 billion. Microsoft's property tax bill? About $14 million. Neighboring Boeing has a market cap of about $40 billion, less than one-tenth that of Microsoft and a real property assessment of $5.5 billion. .. According to Ray Scheppach, executive director of the National Governors Association, "The basic problem is that our tax systems were set up for the manufacturing economy of the 1950s, not a high-tech service-oriented economy."[69]

The problem is more complex. Nicolas Colin, author of a controversial report commissioned by the French Government about the tax system and the digital economy writes, "The digital revolution is old news now, yet only lately have most people begun to get a *feel* of its full implications. As it becomes mainstream, the digital economy gets everywhere in our lives. It permeates our days and nights. Inspiring startups or global corporations disrupt entire industries with their intensive use of IT, innovative business models, iterative design, and a powerful leveraging of data originated by user activity. And yet official statistics utterly fail to measure all this. Multi-sided business models with a predominance of free services are one reason for this failure. Our inability to add data as a primary economic category, just like goods and services, is another. The reality may be that much of the value generated by the digital economy is not captured by official statistics, and therefore leaves our countries unnoticed and ends up in the accounts of offshore

companies. To better grasp this economy, we must revise
many assumptions. A first step is to reconsider the role of
data in value creation. In the digital economy, regular and
systematic monitoring of user activity allows companies to
make intensive use of data in all sorts of ways. Indeed, user
data is not exploited only to target advertising. It can also
be leveraged to customize a product, make purchase
recommendations, maximize producer surplus by adjusting
the price, better match supply and demand based on trust
and reputation, measure and improve the performances of
an application through A/B testing and growth hacking,
fuel innovation efforts to ship new applications, and nurture
entire ecosystems with platform-as-a-service business
models. In short, the digital economy turns business into a
Moneyball game, in which leveraging data leads to global
scale development and higher profitability. Because data
can be stored, aggregated and reused in many ways, user
data is in effect put back into the supply chain where it
creates value on the long term. As the value flowing from
user data has a ripple effect on all the sides of business
models, users become part of business operations,
thereby blurring the line that used to separate consumption
from production. As with content creation or customer
support, users tend to replace employees and contractors in
the supply chain. And because users are not paid like
employees (and they do not want to be for fear of
corrupting the product), their "free work" allows tech
companies to reach the highest economies of scale and
massive profitability. In our common effort to reduce
public deficits and invest in the future, giant tech
companies do not pay much. User activity is sustained,

even enhanced, by massive public investments in education, social insurance, or broadband networks. And *they didn't build that.* On the contrary, every big company in the digital economy has a very low global taxation rate. The value of their intangible assets soars because of network effects, but those assets are located in tax havens where they attract most of the profits (since these companies don't pay dividends, they can locate their profits anywhere). Also, in multi-sided business models, it's easy to spread the side that collects data on every domestic market while concentrating the side that makes money in a single country from where the profits are easier to transfer towards tax havens. Meanwhile, the tax law has not kept up. According to international tax laws, corporate profits should be taxed where corporations have their headquarters. In the digital economy, it's easy to choose a headquarters' location based on where the taxation rate is the lowest. Only when there's a permanent establishment, can a country without a headquarters levy a corporate tax. But the definition of a permanent establishment is gravely out-dated and completely misses the digital economy."[70]

Here it is not possible to go into the full implications (both positive and negative) of the development of this new economy and society, and into the contradictions inherent in this mode. However, before winding up this description a few points should be made clear.

i. This new economy did not evolve by resolving the contradictions inherent in capital. Instead it developed along with (and besides) those contradictions. (Agrarian societies did not emerge by resolving the contradictions inherent in the tribal system, and industrial societies did not develop by resolving the contradictions inherent in the agrarian system. Contradictions inherent in the earlier societies do play their role in the evolution of new modes of production, but they are not the sole factor.)

ii. Transition from hunting-gathering tribal societies to agrarian societies was accomplished through Neolithic revolution which, according to V Gordon Childe, went on for two thousand years. Transition from feudal agrarian society to capitalist society took almost four hundred years (from 14th to 17th century) in case of England. To describe the transition from capitalist industrial society to knowledge society, I am tempted to borrow a term from Hegelian dialectics – **sublation**, a simultaneous cancelling and preservation of something. It best describes the current relationship between suspension and reinforcement of exchange, between free time and labor time. After Empire of Land and Empire of Capital, we are in an age that seeks to create **Empire of the Mind**.[71]

E. Free time and 'Logic of Rights': If capital/income ratio (β) is 6 (that is, total capital is the equivalent of six years of national income), then it means that six years of free time is trapped in capital, and hence, there will be movement to extricate this free time from the clutches of capital. In other words, there will be demands for further reduction of labor time, and therefore, extension of free time.

Moreover, there will also be demands for bringing a number of goods and services out from the fold of exchange – in other words, for free access to a certain number of goods and services as a matter of right. Right to food, right to education, right to health, right to information, right to digital access, etc. do mean free food, free education, free health services, free internet services, etc. Acceptance of these rights means that in case of denial, people have the right to rebel for these free goods and services. Obviously, there will be demands for taking more and more goods and services out of exchange and made free. Popular movements around such rights can be witnessed all over the world.

Needless to say, that since exchange-based economy exists side by side, lots of distortions, leakages, complications, etc. arise; yet, the very acceptance of the principle of free access to a certain number of goods and services is here important. Piketty calls it 'modern redistribution built around logic of rights'. (Part Four/Chapter Thirteen/A Social State for the Twenty-First Century)

Here, one needs to understand the nature of various 'free' internet services – the user, in such cases, by virtue of his very presence and his activities on the net, pays for them 'by supplying data to be exploited by persons unknown to him, in ways that further shape the information being offered to him.'[72]

F. Rise of China: "The combination of a huge population and an extremely high economic growth rate is providing the world with a completely new kind of experience: China is, quite literally, changing the world before our very eyes, taking it into completely uncharted territory. Such is the enormity of this shift and its impact on the world that one might talk of modern economic history being divided into BC and AC – Before China and After China – with 1978 being the great watershed." It may still be premature to go with Martin Jacques's above assessment, but there is no denying the fact that the spectacular rise of China is one of the most defining developments of our age and is sure to greatly influence the shape of things to come in the current century. Much has been written on this subject and therefore I will not go into the growth statistics of contemporary China. On the impact and implications of China's (combined with some other emerging economies') growth story, it will, here, suffice to quote Martin Jacques again:

"The fact that China derives from utterly different civilizational and historical roots to those of the West, and is possessed of quite different geographical co-ordinates, will greatly accentuate the Western sense of loss, disorientation and malaise. It was one thing for Britain to have been confronted with the United States – given the obvious affinities and commonalities that they enjoyed – as its rival and successor as the world's dominant power, but it is an entirely different matter for the United States to be faced with China – with whom it has nothing in common in either civilizational or political terms – as its usurper and ultimate replacement. For the United States, the shock of no longer having the world to itself – what has amounted to a proprietorial right to determine what happens on all major global questions – will be profound. With the rise of China, Western universalism will cease to be universal – and its value and outlook will become steadily less influential. The emergence of China as a global power in effect relativizes everything. The West is habituated to the idea that the world is **its** world, the international community **its** community, the international institutions **its** institutions, the world currency – namely the dollar – **its** currency, and the world's language – namely English – **its** language. The assumption has been that the adjective 'Western' naturally and implicitly belongs in front of each important noun. That will no longer be the case. The West will progressively discover, to its acute discomfort, that the world is no longer Western. .."[73]

There are, of course, some other important developments that have been left here (Piketty discusses some of them like ecological and environmental questions).

Piketty's book does not, in the main, consider these major developments of the twentieth century that are playing vital role in shaping the economy and society in the twenty-first century. He desists from entering **new time**. Hence, the **content** of the book does not justify the **title** 'Capital in the Twenty-First Century'. Given the subject matter of the book, the appropriate title should have been '**Inequality in the Age of Capital**'.

No book is complete and free from certain inconsistencies. Some incompleteness, certain inconsistencies are part of a book – it keeps the door of fresh explorations, interpretations and explanations open for those who want to pursue the subject further. What I am emphasizing is the basic inconsistencies (in the propositions and arguments) of the book.

6. YES MARX NO MARX

For if it is rash to walk into a lion's den unarmed, rash to navigate the
Atlantic in a rowing boat, rash to stand on one foot on the top of St
Paul's, it is still more rash to go home alone with a poet. A poet is
Atlantic and lion in one. While one drowns us the other gnaws us. If we
survive the teeth, we succumb to the waves. A man who can destroy
illusions is both beast and flood.

Virginia Woolf; 'Orlando: A Biography'.[74]

Since the publication of the Volume I of Marx's **Capital**
one hundred forty seven years ago (in September, 1867),
economists have been trying to (some even claiming to)
find an answer to Marx and have been miserably failing in
this task. Yet the tradition is being zealously maintained.

During the last decades of the nineteenth century
(particularly from 1870s to 1890s), feverish attempts were
made to clear the economic field of any trace of the
classical theory of labor value, and particularly of Marx's
theory of surplus value. What remained after this clearing
was '**pure economics**' secured within the circles of a few
schools – the **Austrian School** (Carl Menger, Friederich
von Wieser, and Eugen Böhm-Bawerk), the **Mathematical
School** (Léon Walras and William S Jevons), the
American School (John B Clark), and the **Cambridge
School** (A Marshall and Arthur C Pigou).

In the 1920s, in an attempt to find an answer to Marx, German economist **Werner Sombart** enunciated the theory of social pluralism explaining the evolution of society through co-existence of systems, with each newly emerging systems joining the foregoing one, rather than superseding it. He was just advancing upon another German economist **Adolf von Wagner**'s theory of mixed economy.

In the 1940s, **Joseph Schumpeter** was very much engaged with Marx while writing his '**Capitalism, Socialism and Democracy**'. And in the post-Second World War period, American economists **John Galbraith**, **Pitirim Sorokin** and the Dutch economist **Jan Tinbergen** advocated the **theory of convergence** maintaining that the evolution and inter-penetration of capitalism and socialism will result in the emergence of a so-called universal society, combining the best features of the two socio-economic systems. No need to add that Marx was very much in their minds while they were contemplating on convergence.

However, it is not necessary to go into that history. But it will be quite unfair not to mention **John Maynard Keynes** in this regard. Keynes finds his answer to Marx in the person of 'the strange, unduly neglected prophet **Silvio Gesell** (1862-1930)'. He writes:

"Gesell was a successful German merchant in Buenos Aires who was led to the study of monetary problems by the crisis of the late eighties, which was especially violent in the Argentine. .. He returned to Switzerland in 1906 as a man of some means, able to devote the last decades of his life to the two most delightful occupations open to those who do not have to earn their living, authorship and experimental farming. ... The first section of his standard work was published in 1906 (at Les Hauts Geneveys, Switzerland) under the title 'Die Verwirklichung des Rechtes auf dem vollen Arbeitsertrag', and the second section in 1911 at Berlin under the title 'Die neue Lehre vom Zins'. The two together were published in Berlin and in Switzerland during the war (1916), .. the English version .. being called '**The Natural Economic Order**'. In April 1919 Gesell joined the short-lived **Soviet cabinet of Bavaria as their Minister of Finance**, being subsequently tried by court-martial. The last decade of his life was spent in Berlin and Switzerland and devoted to propaganda. Gesell, drawing to himself the semi-religious fervor which had formerly centered around Henry George, became the revered prophet of a cult with many thousand disciples throughout the world. The first international convention of the Swiss and German Freiland-Freigeld Bund and similar organizations from many countries was held in Basle in 1923. Since his death in 1930 much of the peculiar type of fervor which doctrines such as his are capable of exciting has been diverted to other (in my opinion less eminent) prophets. Dr Buchi is the leader of the movement in England, but its literature seems to be distributed from San Antonio, Texas, its main strength lying today in the United States, where Professor Irving Fisher, alone amongst academic economists, has recognized its significance.

In spite of the prophetic trappings with which his devotees have decorated him, Gesell's main book is written in cool, scientific language; though it is suffused throughout by a more passionate, a more emotional devotion to social justice than some think decent in a scientist. The part which derives from Henry George, though doubtless an important source of the movement's strength, is of altogether secondary interest. The **purpose of the book** as a whole may be described as the **establishment of an anti-Marxian socialism**, a reaction against **laissez-faire** built on theoretical foundations totally unlike those of Marx in being based on repudiation instead of on an acceptance of the classical hypotheses, and on an unfettering of competition instead of its abolition. **I BELIEVE THAT THE FUTURE WILL LEARN MORE FROM THE SPIRIT OF GESELL THAN FROM THAT OF MARX**. The preface to the 'The Natural Economic Order' will indicate to the reader, if he will refer to it, the moral quality of Gesell. **The answer to Marxism is, I think, to be found along the lines of this preface.**"[75]

Contrary to Keynes' wishes, today no one (including Mr Piketty) remembers Gesell and his preface to 'The Natural Economic Order'. Gesell is forgotten, but Marx still continues to preoccupy the minds of twenty-first century economists.

Marx's long shadow is quite apparent in Thomas Piketty's book from beginning to end. At every point, before propounding his conclusions, he remembers and cites Marx, but quickly backtracks. He strives hard to find an answer to Marx, but fails. He is not the first to do so, and not the last to fail. In the earlier parts of this critique, I have already dealt with the 'Yes Marx No Marx' syndrome of Mr Piketty, and hence, no further elaboration is needed.

However, one complaint remains, and very often mentioned in the book. He says, "He (Marx) no doubt lacked the statistic data needed to refine his predictions. He probably suffered as from having decided on his conclusions in 1848, before embarking on the research needed to justify them. Marx evidently wrote in great political fervor, which at times led him to issue hasty pronouncements from which it was difficult to escape. That is why economic theory needs to be rooted in historical sources that are as complete as possible, and in this respect Marx did not exploit all the possibilities available to him." (Introduction) "To summarize: he (Marx) occasionally sought to make use of the best available statistics of the day (which were better than the statistics available to Malthus and Ricardo but still quite rudimentary), but he usually did so in a rather impressionistic way and without always establishing a clear connection to his theoretical argument." (Introduction/Note 8) Further, "Despite important intuitions, Marx usually adopted a fairly anecdotal and unsystematic approach to the available statistics." (Chapter Six)

Given the conditions under which Marx had to work, and even conceding that he might have missed some available data, anyone who has gone through his writings – Grundrisse, A Contribution to the Critique of Political Economy, three volumes of Capital, Theories of Surplus Value, etc. – will hardly agree with Piketty's observations. Two facts are all too clear – one, Marx rigorously tried to collect and analyze all available statistics to the extent possible, and second, he critically and quite extensively examined almost all the currents of thought then existing. No book of his time comes even close to his voluminous works.

While describing the 'History of the Ricardian Law of Rent' ('Theories of Surplus Value', Part II), he studies and analyses the annual average prices of corn from 1641 to 1859 (quoting Sir Edward West's 'Price of Corn and Wages of Labor', London, 1826). Moreover, in order to gain greater access to available data and literature, he got himself admitted to the Society of Arts and Trades (which was formed in 1754) in May 1869. It gave him access to the Society's library, including the extremely large collection of works by the 17th-19th century economists. Many of them he used when working on Capital.

Marx's economic writings contain very extensive critical examination of almost all the figures of classical political economy – William Petty, Boisguillebert, Benjamin Franklin, François Quesnay, Anderson, Sir James Steuart, Condillac, Adam Smith, Sir F M Eden, Townsend, Wallace, Malthus, Bentham, Ricardo, James and John Stuart Mill, Wilhelm Roscher, George Ramsay, J B Say, Cobbett, Rodbertus, Hopkins, Sismondi, William Carey, Bestiat, etc.

And his great political fervor (in favor of the working class) was invariably accompanied with his relentless struggles against sectarianism.[76] His political fervor did not cloud his vision to the extent that he could not see the objective facts and their historical sources. Contrary to Piketty's observations, see what **Bertrand Russel** has to say about Marx in this regard, ".. **He (Marx) was always anxious to appeal to evidence, and never relied upon any extra-scientific intuition.**"[77]

Marx's 'Capital' was met with a 'conspiracy of silence' and Kugelmann and Engels had to take considerable trouble to blow up this conspiracy. Kugelmann managed to publish anonymously a number of reviews by Engels in various newspapers. But soon, the book got organically linked with working class/socialist/communist movement.

Piketty's book is an instant hit, a bestseller from the very start. I will not go into the marketing strategy of the publishers cashing in on the popular sentiment prevailing in the background of the 'Occupy movement' in the US and anti-austerity movements in Europe. Nothing can be more false and misleading than comparing Marx's 'Capital' with Piketty's 'Capital in the Twenty-First Century', and to call Piketty's book Capital 2.0. To call him 'Modern Marx' or 'Bigger than Marx' is simply ridiculous.

The sound of the book that met with a 'conspiracy of silence' is still reverberating in the ears of 21st century economists. The fate of the book that is a blockbuster from the very start is at present anybody's guess.

It was really rash for Mr Piketty to go home with Karl Marx while writing his book. In that case he should not have hoped to survive the teeth and to avoid succumbing to the waves.

7. LONDON CHICAGO PARIS

The ideas of economists and political philosophers, both when they are right and when they are wrong, are more powerful than is commonly understood. Indeed the world is ruled by little else. Practical men, who believe themselves to be exempt from any intellectual influences, are usually the slaves of some defunct economist. Madmen in authority, who hear voices in the air, are distilling their frenzy from some academic scribbler of a few years back. I am sure that the power of vested interests is vastly exaggerated compared with the gradual encroachment of ideas. Not, indeed, immediately, but after a certain interval; for in the field of economic and political philosophy there are not many who are influenced by new theories after they are twenty-five or thirty years of age, so that the ideas which civil servants and politicians and even agitators apply to current events are not likely to be the newest. But, soon or late, it is ideas, not vested interests, which are dangerous for good or evil.

John Maynard Keynes; 'The General Theory of Employment, Interest and Money', Chapter 24, 'Concluding Notes on the Social Philosophy towards Which The General Theory Might Lead'.[78]

At the beginning of political economy, British, French and American economists and philosophers dominated the scene. A comparative study of their writings and characters illuminates the social divergence among Britain, France and America at the close of the seventeenth century and the beginning of the eighteenth. It explains the origins of the national contrasts obtaining in British, French and American political economies. Here, we may have a quick look into the origin of political economy as a separate discipline.[79]

William Petty (1623-1687): The father of English political economy wrote his 'Political Arithmetick etc.' (London, 1699) at a time when Holland was still the predominant trading nation and France seemed to be on the way to becoming the principal trading power. However, Petty believed and proved that England was destined to conquer the world market: " That the King of England's subjects have stock competent and convenient to drive the trade of the whole commercial world. That the impediments of England's greatness are but contingent and removable." (Holland was then regarded as the model country just as Britain was later regarded as the model country by continental economists.)

Petty treats the division of labor as a productive force, and in his 'Essay Concerning the Multiplication of Mankind etc.' (1698), he shows the advantages which division of labor has for production not only with the example of the manufacture of a watch – as Adam Smith did later with the example of the manufacture of a pin – but considers also a town and a whole country as large-scale industrial establishments. This conception of the source of material wealth leads to the **political arithmetic**, the first form in which political economy is treated as a separate science. ..His audacious genius becomes evident for instance in his proposal to transport all the movables and people of Ireland, and of the Highlands of Scotland ..into the rest of Great Britain. According to him, this would result in the saving of labor time, in increasing productivity of labor, and 'the King and his subjects would thereby become more rich and strong'.

Petty rejects taxes which transfer wealth from industrious people to those who do nothing at all, but eat and drink, sing, play, and dance; nay such as study the Metaphysics'.

About the person, Marx writes, "..William Petty is not only the father of English political economy but also an ancestor of Henry Petty, alias Marquis of Lansdowne, the Nestor of the English Whigs. But the Lansdowne family could hardly prepare a complete edition of Petty's works without prefacing it with his biography, and what is true with regard to the origin of most of the big Whig families, applies also in this case – the less said of it, the better. The army surgeon, who was a bold thinker but quite unscrupulous and just as apt to plunder in Ireland under the aegis of Cromwell as to fawn upon Charles II to obtain the title of baronet to embellish his trash, is hardly a suitable image of an ancestor for public display. In most of the writings published during his lifetime, moreover, Petty seeks to prove that England's golden age was the reign of Charles II, a rather heterodox view for hereditary exploiters of the 'Glorious Revolution'.[80]

Pierre le Pesant, sieur de Boisguillebert (1646-1714): The father of French political economy Boisguillebert wrote his 'Dissertation sur la nature des richnesse de l'argent et des tributs' in an entirely different conditions compared to Britain. He fights against the 'blindly destructive greed for gold which possessed the court of Louis XIV, his tax farmers and the aristocracy; whereas Petty acclaims the greed for gold as a vigorous force which spurs a nation to industrial progress and to the conquest of the world market.

Boisguillebert (although he may not be aware of it) reduces the exchange value of commodities to labor time, by determining the 'true value' according to the correct proportion in which the labor time of the individual producers is divided between the different branches of industry, and declaring that free competition is the social process by which this correct proportion is established. But simultaneously, and in contrast with Petty, he wages a fanatical struggle against money, whose intervention, he alleges, disturbs the natural equilibrium or the harmony of the exchange of commodities and, like a fantastic **Moloch**, demands all physical wealth as a sacrifice.

This difference between Boisguillebert and Petty throws into bold relief more profound fundamental differences which recur as a perpetual contrast between typically English and typically French political economy.

William Petty was just a frivolous, grasping, unprincipled adventurer, Boisguillebert, although he was one of the intendants of Louis XIV, stood up for the interests of the oppressed classes with both great intellectual force and courage.

Benjamin Franklin (1706-1790): Franklin was a man of the New World – where bourgeois relations of production was imported together with their representatives sprouted rapidly in a soil in which the superabundance of humus made up for lack of historical tradition. Among the first supporters of the labor theory of value, Franklin formulated the basic law of modern political economy in an early work written in 1729 and published in 1731 ('A Modest Inquiry into the Nature and Necessity of a Paper Currency').

Sir James Steuart (1712-1780), one of the last representatives of mercantilism, was the first Briton to expound a general system of bourgeois political economy. His work 'An Inquiry into the Principles of Political Economy, Being an Essay on the Science of Domestic Policy in Free Nations' was first published in London in 1767, ten years earlier than Adam Smith's 'Wealth of Nations'. 'Le Commerce et la Gouvernement' of **Etiênne Bonnet de Condillac** (1715-1780) was published in 1776, the same year in which Adam Smith's work was published. Condillac has been dealt with earlier in this critique.

Henry Charles Carey (1793-1879): American economist, for whose views the historical background was provided only by the New World, set forth the theory of class interest's harmony in capitalist society. According to him, the harmonies **in themselves** are there. But in the non-American countries they are distorted by the state, and in America itself, by the most developed form in which these relationships appear, their world-market reality, in the form of England. Carey finds no other means of restoring them than ultimately to call for help from his denounced devil, the state, and to stand it as the guardian angel at the gates of the harmonious paradise, namely protective tariffs. But since America's development over the years has dealt such a blow at his harmonious view that he sees the distortion of the 'natural' harmonies, to which he is firmly attached, no longer in the external influence of the state, but in trade! A truly remarkable result this: to extol exchange value as the basis of harmonious production, and then to declare that the developed form of exchange, trade, abolishes this exchange value in its immanent laws! That is the desperate form in which Carey expresses his belated conclusion that the development of harmonious exchange value is disharmonic. ..

Frédéric Bastiat (1801-1850), the French economist borrowed his economic theodicy, the **Harmonies économiques** from Carey. But Bastiat's only real background was the pettiness of French economic conditions, whose long years kept sticking out from his harmonies, and in contrast to these, he formulated the idealized English and American production relationships as 'the demands of practical reason'.

Here I do not want to prolong this description of early classical political economy. Suffice it to say that soon **Adam Smith** and his 'Wealth of Nations' became the representative symbol of the classical political economy. The rise of Britain as the paramount industrial and colonial power helped in this process. French and American streams were relegated to the background.

Marx's 'Capital' (as its sub-title proclaimed) **was the critique of political economy**. This critique soon became the guiding spirit behind the working class movement, and this critique was further carried forward by the social-democratic/socialist/communist movements. If one (like Piketty) wants to revive the spirit of political economy, he/she is bound to encounter the spirit of the critique of political economy as well. If political economy faces the

challenge of entering new time, then the critique of political economy too faces the same challenge. Mere revival will not do.

We have already seen that between the period 1870s-1920s, the various streams of Austrian School dominated the bourgeois economic scene. Rest of the twentieth century was dominated by the **London School** (Keynes) and the **Chicago School** (Milton Friedman). The period 1930s-1970s was dominated by various streams of Keynesian economics, and the latter period (from 1980s onwards) by various proponents of the Chicago School.

Piketty describes the rise of the American school in the 1970s as follows: "It was not until the 1970s Solow's so-called neoclassical growth model definitely carried the day ..as American economists sought to emancipate themselves from the historical tutelage of their British counterparts, who had reigned over the profession since the time of Adam Smith, while the British sought to defend the memory of Lord Keynes, which they thought the American economists had betrayed." (Chapter Six/Beyond the Two Cambridges)

But where were the French?

École d'Économie de Paris (Paris School of Economics) is a fairly new institute, created just eight years ago on December 21, 2006 in Paris. Its tagline is 'Economics serving society', and its brochure pledges to shake up economics:

"The central paradigm of economic science, according to which man is a rational economic agent, has provided powerful explanations of a number of social phenomena. However it today faces numerous challenges: the increasing complexity of those phenomena, an explosion in available data, scientific experimentation. In this context, there are now three main possible approaches to studying economics: the first is to deepen the existing paradigm for certain kinds of question, the second is to critically re-examine that paradigm and seek alternatives to remedy its failures; the third possible path is to investigate the boundaries shared by economics and other social sciences (history, demographics, sociology, social psychology, political science) and other disciplines (including neuroscience and cognitive science).

Thanks to its pluralism, PSE is at the forefront of this evolution in economic thinking, using an approach that is both traditional and innovative to investigate the open questions in economics. For instance, our researchers ask how we should manage economic activity and regulate the global economic cycle, especially during periods of crisis; how to reduce poverty in developing countries; how to explain and combat growing inequality; how to evaluate and improve public policy in sectors such as health, the environment and education; or how to model bounded rationality."[81]

Piketty's book strives to follow the brochure's agenda, and hence, it may be aimed at creating **an identity** (distinct from the London and Chicago Schools) for this twenty-first century French school. Can it lift the French school of political economy from centuries of oblivion? Can this school emancipate French economists from the tutelage of their American counterparts?

Remember, in this century different streams of economic thought emanating from emerging economies like China, India, Brazil, etc. will claim their share of economic discourse. Piketty keeps the dialogue confined, in the main, to Europe and the United States.

All said, Thomas Piketty still deserves many thanks.

8. THANK YOU MR PIKETTY

A book must be the axe for the frozen sea within us.

Kafka.

Thank you, Mr Piketty for unequivocally drawing attention to certain realities (substantiated by data spread over two centuries) that provide enough lessons for emerging economies. Of course for India too where the ruling dispensation, backed by the Chicago school enthusiasts, is pushing through a spate of neo-liberal reforms in the interests of the top centile, accompanied with a regressive, divisive Hindutva agenda. I have already quoted many passages from the book, still some more may be the best way to end this critique:

-   **The distribution of wealth is too important an issue to be left to economists, sociologists, and philosophers. It is of interest to everyone, and that is a good thing. The concrete, physical reality of inequality is visible to the naked eye. ..Democracy will never be supplanted by a republic of experts – and that is a very good thing. Classical political economy was born in England and France in the late eighteenth and early nineteenth century, the issue of distribution was already one of the key questions. ..Whenever one speaks about the** distribution of wealth, politics is never very far behind, and it is difficult for anyone to escape contemporary class prejudices and interests.

- One conclusion is already quite clear; it is an illusion to think that something about the nature of modern growth or the laws of market economy ensures that inequality of wealth will decrease and harmonious stability will be achieved.
- There is no natural, spontaneous process to prevent destabilizing, inegalitarian forces from prevailing permanently. ..In any event, it is important to point out that no self-corrective mechanism exists to prevent a steady increase of the capital/income ratio, together with a steady rise in capital's share of national income.
- The very notion of individual marginal productivity becomes hard to define. In fact, it becomes something close to a pure ideological construct on the basis of which a justification for higher status can be elaborated.
- Today, in the second decade of the twenty-first century, inequalities of wealth are close to regaining or even surpassing their historical highs.
- The world to come may well combine the worst of two past worlds: both very large inequality of inherited wealth and very high wage inequalities justified in terms of merit and productivity (claims with little factual basis). Meritocratic extremism can thus lead to a race between supermanagers and rentiers, to the detriment of those who are neither.

- The fundamental force of divergence, which has nothing to do with market imperfections and will not disappear as markets become free and more competitive. The idea that unrestricted competition will put an end to inheritance and move toward a more meritocratic world is a dangerous illusion. The advent of universal suffrage and the end of property qualifications for voting, ended the legal domination of politics by the wealthy. But it did not abolish the economic forces capable of producing a society of rentiers.
- New forms of organization and ownership remain to be invented.
- Real democracy and social justice require specific institutions of their own, not just those of the market, and not just parliaments and other formal democratic institutions.

Thank you Mr Piketty.

PERSONALITIES

IN CHRONOLOGICAL ORDER

1. **William Petty** (1623-1687): English economist and statistician; founder of the classical school of political economy in Britain.

2. **Pierre le Pesant, sieur de Boisguillebert** (1646-1714): Founder of French political economy.

3. **John Law** (1671-1729): Scottish economist, banker, merchant, founder of the first Bank of France. He is held responsible for the 'Mississipi Bubble'.

4. **Richard Cantillon** (1680-1734): An Irish-French economist, Physiocrat, influenced by William Petty, John Locke and Isaac Newton. His book 'Esssai sur la Nature du Commerce en Général' greatly influenced Quesnay, Steuart and Adam Smith.

5. **François Quesnay** (1694-1774): French physician and economist; founder of the Physiocratic School.

6. **Robert Wallace** (1697-1771): British clergyman, author of several works on population questions, some of his ideas were taken over by Malthus.

7. **Claude-Jacques Herbert** (1700-1758): French economist, one of the forerunners of Malthus's population theory.

8. **Benjamin Franklin** (1706-1790): American physicist, economist and politician.

9. **James Steuart** (1712-1780): One of the last representatives of mercantilism, was the first Briton to expound a general system of classical political economy. His work 'An Inquiry into the Principles of Political Economy, Being an Essay on the Science of Domestic Polity in Free Nations' was first published in London in 1767, ten years earlier than Adam Smith's 'Wealth of Nations'.

10. **Etiênne Bonnet de Condillac** (1715-1780): French economist and philosopher; follower of Locke. His 'Le Commerce et la Gouvernement' was published in 1776, the year Adam Smith published his 'Wealth of Nations'. He is considered as the predecessor of the utility theorists of the nineteenth century.

11. **Adam Smith** (1723-1790): Scottish economist, one of the great representatives of the classical political economy. His 'Wealth of Nations' (1776) still remains one of the most influential works on capitalist economy.

12. **James Anderson** (1739-1808): British economist, a forerunner of Ricardo's in the theory of rent.

13. **Joseph Townsend** (1739-1816): Clergyman, geologist and sociologist; worked out a population theory which was largely used by Malthus.

14. **Marie Jean Antoine Nicolas de Caritat, marquis de Condorcet** (1743-1794): French philosopher, mathematician, economist and political scientist. He worked with Leonard Euler and Benjamin Franklin. His social choice theory influenced twentieth century economists like Kenneth Arrow and Amartya Sen.

15. **Jeremy Bentham** (1748-1832): English philosopher and founder of utilitarianism.

16. **Thomas Robert Malthus** (1766-1834): English priest, economist, put forward a theory of population.

17. **Jean Baptiste Say** (1767-1832): French economist.

18. **David Ricardo** (1772-1823): English economist; the last great representative of classical political economy.

19. **James Mill** (1773-1836): Scottish historian, philosopher and economist; follower of Ricardo.

20. **Jean-Charles-Leonard Sismonde de Sismondi** (1773-1842): Swiss historian and economist.

21. **Edward West** (1782-1828): British economist; one of the first to write on the theory of rent.

22. **Henry Charles Carey** (1793-1879): American economist; set forth the theory of class interests' harmony in capitalist society.

23. **George Ramsay** (1800-1871): British philosopher and economist.

24. **Frédéric Bastiat** (1801-1850): French economist; influenced by Carey's theory of harmony of class interests.

25. **Johann Karl Rodbertus** (1805-1875): Prussian landowner and economist; theoretician of the Prussian Junker 'State Socialism'.

26. **John Stuart Mill** (1806-1873): British philosopher and economist, son of James Mill.

27. **Wilhelm Georg Friedrich Roscher** (1817-1894): German economist; the main origins of the historical school of political economy may be traced to him.

28. **Karl Marx** (1818-1883): German philosopher, economist and revolutionary socialist. Author of 'Capital: A Critique of Political Economy' (Volume I, 1867; two subsequent volumes were published after his death).

29. **Léon Walras** (1834-1910): A French mathematical economist; formulated the marginal theory of value and pioneered the development of general equilibrium theory.

30. **William Stanley Jevons** (1835-1882): English logician and economist. His book 'The Theory of Political Economy' (1871) expounded the marginal utility theory of value.

31. **Carl Menger** (1840-1921): Austrian economist and founder of the Austrian school of economics; contributed to the theory of marginalism.

32. **Alfred Marshal** (1842-1924): One of the most prominent economists of his time; combined the ideas of supply and demand, marginal utility and costs of production; his book 'Principles of Economics' was the dominant text-book of economics in England for many years.

33. **John Bates Clark** (1847-1938): American neo-classical economist; one of the pioneers of the marginal productivity theory.

34. **Eugen Böhm von Bawerk** (1851-1914): Austrian economist; made important contributions to the development of the Austrian school of economics.

35. **Friedrich von Wieser** (1851-1926): Early economist of the Austrian school of economics.

36. **Arthur Cecil Pigou** (1877-1959): English economist noted for his studies in welfare economics.

37. **Joseph Schumpeter** (1883-1950): Austrian born American economist; briefly served as the Finance Minister of Austria in 1919; 'creative destruction' is a term coined by him in his work 'Capitalism, Socialism and Democracy'.

38. **John Maynard Keynes** (1883-1946): English economist whose ideas fundamentally changed the theory and practice of macroeconomics; advocated state intervention in economic affairs, a 'mild inflation to fight stagnation'; his work 'The General Theory of Employment, Interest and Money' (1936) influenced the course of world economy for nearly three decades.

39. **Alvin Hansen** (1887-1975): American economist known as 'American Keynes'.

40. **Piero Sraffa** (1898-1983): Italian economist, representative of the neo-Ricardian school of economics.

41. **Michal Kalecki** (1899-1970): Polish economist, specialized in macroeconomics; invented the theory of effective demand.

42. **Henry Roy Forbes Harrod** (1900-1978): English economist; contributed to the field of macroeconomics and known for the development of Harrod-Domar model.

43. **Simon Kuznets** (1901-1985): American economist, statistician, demographer and economic historian; awarded Nobel Prize in economics in 1971.

44. **Joan Robinson** (1903-1983): British economist, well-known for her work on monetary economics and wide-ranging contributions to economic theory.

45. **John Richard Hicks** (1904-1989): British economist; one of the most important and influential economists of the 20th century.

46. **Nicholas Kaldor** (1908-1986): Cambridge economist.

47. **Milton Friedman** (1912-2006): American economist known for his research on consumption analysis, monetary history and theory and complexity of stabilization policy; won Nobel Prize in 1976.

48. **Evsey Domar** (1914-1997): Russian-American economist well-known as co-author of Harrod-Domar model; a leading theorist of economic growth and expert on comparative economic systems.

49. **Paul Samuelson** (1915-2009): American economist, first American to win the Nobel Prize in Economic Sciences in 1970.

50. **Robert Merton Solow** (1924-): American economist particularly known for his work on the theory of economic growth.

51. **Luigi Pasinetti** (1930-): Italian economist of the post-Keynesian school.

52. **Alex Leijonhufvud** (1933-): Swedish economist, Professor Emeritus at University of California Los Angeles (UCLA) and Professor at the University of Trento, Italy; influenced Greek economist and politician, Yanis Varoufakis.

NOTES

1. Selected Works of Virginia Woolf; 'Orlando: A Biography', Wordsworth Editions Limited, Hertfordshire, 2005.

2. Proust, Marcel; 'In Search of Lost Time 6', 'Finding Time Again', Penguin Books, London, 2002. Translated from the French by Ian Patterson.

3. Mann, Thomas; 'The Magic Mountain', Vintage Books, London, 1999. Translated from the German by H T Lowe-Porter. Quotations have been selected from different pages of the novel.

4. Ibid.

5. Piketty, Thomas; 'Capital in the Twenty-First Century', The Belknap Press of Harvard University Press, Cambridge, Massachusetts, London, 2014. Translated from the French by Arthur Goldhammer. (From now on, references – related chapters and subheadings - regarding all the quotations of Thomas Piketty from this book will be mentioned in the running text in bracket.)

6. Mayer-Schönberger, Viktor, and Cukier, Kenneth; 'Big data', John Murray, London, 2013.

7. Ibid.

8. Ibid.

9. Sen, Amartya; 'The Idea of Justice', Allen Lane, London. 2009.

10. Engels, Frederick; 'Anti-Duhring', Foreign Languages Press, Peking, 1976.

11. "In the Preface to Sir Dudley North's 'Discourses upon Trade' (1691) it is stated that **Descartes' method** had begun to free Political

Economy from the old fables and superstitious notions of gold, trade, &c. On the whole, however, the early English economists sided with **Bacon** and **Hobbes** as their philosophers; while at a later period, the philosopher of Political Economy in England, France and Italy was **Locke**." Karl Marx, 'Capital', Volume I, Part IV (Continued), Chapter XV, Section 2, Second Footnote, p. 368. Progress Publishers, Moscow, 1977. Translated from the third German edition by **Samuel Moore** and **Edward Aveling**.

12. Foucault, Michel; 'The Archaeology of Knowledge', Routledge Classics, Oxon, 2006.

13. Quoted by Karl Marx, 'Capital', Volume III, Chapter XXIV, p. 393. Progress Publishers, Moscow, 1977.

14. Marx, Karl, and Engels, Frederick; Collected Works, Volume 43, Progress Publishers, Moscow, 1988. Marx to Ludwig Kugelmann, London, 11 July, 1868. "The vulgar economist thinks he had made a great discovery when, faced with the disclosure of the intrinsic interconnection, he insists that things look different in appearance. **In fact, he prides himself in his clinging to appearances and believing them to be the ultimate. Why then have science at all?**"

15. **Economist**, London, July 19, 1851. Quoted by Marx in 'Capital', Volume I, Part VII, Chapter XXIV.

16. Ibid. Quotations are from different chapters and pages of the book.

17. Ibid.

18. Ibid.

19. Marx, Karl; 'Capital', Volume III, Progress Publishers, Moscow, 1977.

20. Ramsay, George; 'An Essay on the Distribution of Wealth', Edinburg, 1836. Quoted in Karl Marx's 'Capital', Volume III, p.362.

21. Ibid.

22. Ibid.

23.Ibid.

24. Ibid.

25. Ibid. Moloch: the god of sun, fire and war in Carthage and Phoenicia, whose worship was accompanied by human sacrifices.

26. Ibid.

27. Ibid.

28. Quoted in Marx's 'Capital', Volume I, Progress Publishers, Moscow, 1977.

29. Marx, Karl and Engels, Frederick; Collected Works, Volume 29, Progress Publishers, Moscow, 1987.

30. Boisguillebert, 'Dissertation sur la nature des richesses, de l'argent et des tributs', Daire edition. Quoted in Marx, 'Original Text of A Contribution to the Critique of Political Economy', Chapter Two, 'Money'. Karl Marx- Frederick Engels Collected Works, Volume 29, Progress Publishers, Moscow, 1987.

31. Marx, Karl; 'Capital', Volume I, Chapter V, 'Contradictions in the General Formula of Capital', Moscow, 1977.

32. Ibid.

33. Marx-Engels Collected Works; Volume 29, Moscow, 1977.

34. Marx, Karl; 'Capital', Volume I (details already mentioned in previous notes).

35. Ibid. See also V I Lenin's article 'Marx-Engels'.

36. Ibid.

37. Cohen-Bendit, Daniel and Cohen-Bendit, Gabriel; 'Obsolete Communism: The Left-Wing Alternative', Andre Deutsch, London, 1968. Translated by Arnold Pomerans.

38. Marx to Kugelmann, December 12, 1868. Marx-Engels Collected Works, Volume 29.

39. Marx, 'Capital', Volume I.

40. Marx to Meyer and Vogt, April 9, 1870. Marx-Engels Collected Works, Volume 29.

41. Marx; 'Manufactures and Commerce', London, September 5, 1859. Marx-Engels Collected Works, Volume 16.

42. Marx, 'Crime and Pauperism', London, August 23, 1859. Marx-Engels Collected Works, Volume 16.

43. Marx-Engels Collected Works, Volume 29.

44. Rajan, Raghuram and Zingales, Luigi; 'Saving Capitalism from the Capitalists', Crown Business, New York, 2003.

45. Total Factor Productivity: It is a component of growth in the value of goods and services produced by an economy that is left over after accounting for the increased use of capital and labor. It is based on the theory of marginal productivity. TFP of any entity is the difference between what it produces and what it uses as inputs. For a country, output is gross domestic product (GDP) while inputs are the capital used, employed labor, the skill level of the employed labor, etc. For the past three decades the Centre for the International Comparisons of Production, Income and Prices at the University of Pennsylvania has been compiling internationally comparable data for a number of countries. Its latest data release is the PWT 8.0, which was released recently. For India, the data is as follows: Between 1960 and 1991, the economy grew at an average annual rate of 4.3%. This growth rate rose to 6.8% between 1991 and 2011. Correspondingly, TFP growth in India which averaged 0.65% a year between 1960 and 1991 almost tripled to 1.64% between 1991 and 2011. Put differently, while TFP growth accounted for about 15% of annual GDP growth during 1960-1991, it

accounted for 24% of the higher GDP growth during 1991-2011. (The Times of India, May 7, 2014; article by Amartya Lahiri.)

46. Rajan, Raghuram and Zingales, Luigi; 'Saving Capitalism from the Capitalists', Crown Business, New York, 2003.

47. Ibid.

48. Marx, 'Capital', Volume I. Marx: "I must remind the reader that the categories, 'variable and constant capital', were first used by me. Political Economy since the time of Adam Smith has confusedly mixed up the essential distinctions involved in these categories, with the mere formal differences, arising out of the process of circulation, of fixed and circulating capital." The rate of profit [s/(c+v)] is always less than the rate of surplus value [s/v]. Where the organic composition c/v is 50/100, a rate of surplus value of 100% is expressed in a rate of profit of $66^2/_3$%, and at a higher stage, where c/v is 400/100, the same rate of surplus value is expressed in a rate of profit of only 20%. What is true of different successive stages of development in one country, is also true of different co-existing stages of development in different countries. In an underdeveloped country, in which the former composition of capital is the average, the general rate of profit would = $66^2/_3$%, while in a country with the latter composition and a much higher stage of development, it would = 20%.

49. Marx, 'Capital', Volume III.

50. Virgil; 'The Aeneid', Book Third; The Modern Library, Random House, New York, 1950. Translated by J W Mackail.

51. Woolf, Virginia; 'Orlando: A Biography', Selected Works of Virginia Woolf, Wordsworth Editions Limited, Hertfordshire, 2005.

52. Rajan, Raghuram G, and Zingales, Luigi; 'Saving Capitalism from the Capitalists', Crown Business, New York, 2003.

53. Marx, Karl; 'Capital', Volume I, Chapter XXIV.

54. Marx-Engels Collected Works; Volume 43. ('Doctrine de Saint-Simon Exposition', Première année, 1829, Paris. 1830.)

55. Ibid.

56. Hobsbawm, Eric; 'The Age of Capital, 1848-1885', New American Library, New York, 1979.

57. Chandler, Alfred; 'Scale and Scope: The Dynamics of Industrial Capitalism', Cambridge, Massachusetts, Belknap Press, 1990. Quoted in Rajan and Zingales.

58. Rajan and Zingales; op.cit.

59. Twain, Mark; 'Huckleberry Finn', Paragon Boks, London, 1994.

60. Ibsen, Henrik; 'Three Plays', 'The Pillars of the Community', Penguin Books, London, 1954. Translated by Una Ellis-Fermor.

61. Marx, Karl; 'The Civil War in France', Foreign Languages Press, Peking, 1966.

62. Nicholl, Charles; 'Leonardo da Vinci', Penguin Books, London, 2007.

63. Voltaire; 'Candide and Other Tales', 'Master Simple', Heron Books, Geneva, 1969. Translation by Tobias Smollett.

64. Marx, Karl; 'Grundrisse: Foundations of the Critique of Political Economy' (Rough Draft), Penguin Books in association with New Left Review, Harmondsworth, Middlesex, England, 1981. Translated with a Foreword by Martin Nicolaus.

65. Stewart, Thomas A; 'The Wealth of Knowledge: Intellectual Capital and the 21st Century Organization', Part I, 'The Theory of a Knowledge Business', Currency Doubleday (a division of Random House Inc.), 2001.

66. Rodrik, Dani; 'Democracy and the Future of the World Economy: Globalization Paradox', W W Norton, 2011. Rodrik writes, "Adam Smith's idealized market society required little more than a 'night-watchman state'. All that governments needed to do to ensure the division of labor was to enforce property rights, keep the peace, and

collect a few taxes to pay for a limited range of public goods such as national defense. Through the early part of the twentieth century and the first wave of globalization, capitalism was governed by a narrow vision of the public institutions needed to uphold it. .. Let us call this '**Capital 1.0**'. 'The mixed-economy model' (Keynesian economy) was the crowning achievement of the twentieth century. .. (It was) '**Capital 2.0**' with a limited kind of globalization – the Bretton Woods compromise." Rodrik, then, enunciates principles for a New Globalization of '**Capital 3.0**': i. Markets must be deeply embedded in systems of governance; ii. Democratic government and political communities are organized largely within nation states, and are likely to remain so for the immediate future; iii. There is no 'one way' to prosperity; iv. Countries have the right to protect their own social arrangements, regulations, and institutions; v. Countries do not have the right to impose their institutions on others; vi. The purpose of international economic arrangements must be to lay down the traffic rules for managing the interface among national institutions; and vii. Non-democratic countries cannot count on the same rights and privileges in the international economic order as democracies. .. "The key to capitalism's durability lies in its almost infinite malleability. As our conceptions of the institutions needed to support markets and economic activity have evolved over the centuries, so has capitalism. Thanks to its capacity for re-invention, capitalism has overcome its periodic crises and outlived its critics, from Karl Marx on. .."

67. Kissinger, Henry; 'World Order: Reflections on the Character of Nations and the Course of History', Penguin Press, New York, 2014.

68. Assange, Julian; 'Google Is Not What It Seems', wikileaks.org/google-is-not-what-it-seems/

69. Stewart, Thomas A; op.cit.

70. Colin, Nicolas; 'Corporate Tax 2.0: Why France and the World Need a New Tax System for the Digital Age', http://www.forbes.com/sites/singularity/2013/01/28/corporate-tax-2-0-why-france-and-the-world-need-a-new-tax-system-for-the-digital-age/

71. Assange, Julian; op.cit. **'The Empire of the Mind'** was the working title of the book written by Google Chairman Eric Schmidt and Jared Cohen, the Director of Google Ideas. The book was eventually published in April 2013. The working title was replaced with **'The New Digital Age: Reshaping the Future of People, Nations and Business'**.

72. Kissinger, Henry; op.cit.

73. Jacques, Martin; 'When China Rules the World: The End of the Western World and the Birth of a New Global Order', The Penguin Press, New York, 2009.

74. Virginia Woolf; op.cit.

75. Keynes, John Maynard; 'The General Theory of Employment, Interest and Money' (1936), Chapter 23, 'Notes on Mercantilism, The Usury Laws, Stamped Money and Theories of Under-consumption'. A Project Gutenberg of Australia eBook, February 2003. This eBook was produced by Col Choat: colc@gutenberg.net.au

76. In his letter to the Lassallean Johann Baptist von Schweitzer (October 13, 1868), Marx wrote, "The sect seeks its **raison d'être** and its **point d'honneur** not in what it has **in common** with the class movement but in the **particular shibboleth distinguishing** it from that movement. ..Yet instead you, in fact, demanded that the **class movement subordinated itself to a particular sect movement.** Your non-friends concluded from this that you wished to conserve your 'own workers' movement under all circumstances." Marx-Engels Collected Works, Volume 43; op.cit.

77. Russel, Bertrand; 'History of Western Philosophy', George Allen and Unwin Ltd., London, 1967.

78. Keynes, John Maynard; op.cit.

79. Descriptions regarding the beginning of political economy are taken from and based on Marx's 'A Contribution to the Critique of Political Economy', Part One, (Written in November 1858-January 1859) and 'Grundrisse'; op.cit.

80. Ibid. The 'Glorious Revolution': the coup d'état of 1688-89, as a result of which the Stuart James II was overthrown and William III of Orange was proclaimed King of England. It led to a limitation of the King's powers in the interests of the commercial and financial bourgeoisie and the circles of the landed aristocracy connected with them.

81. From the Brochure of École d'Économie de Paris.

October, 2014.

****

19591510R00094

Printed in Great Britain
by Amazon